THOMAS WAKLEY

An Improbable Radical

Thomas Wakley

An Improbable Radical

by

John Hostettler

BA, LLB (Hons), LLM, PhD (London)
Solicitor of the Supreme Court

Published by
Barry Rose Law Publishers Ltd.
Little London
Chichester

Also published by the same author

The Politics of Criminal Law -
Reform in the Nineteenth Century

ISBN 1 872328 90 3

The Ballot reproduced by kind permission of the Newspaper
Library, Colindale

The front page, of the first issue of The Lancet is published by
permission of the British Library

THOMAS WAKLEY -
AN IMPROBABLE RADICAL

CONTENTS

PREFACE

Thomas Wakley was a man who aroused conflicting emotions of affection and aversion throughout his tempestuous life. His restless energy emerged in the first half of a nineteenth century distinguished by discordant contrasts of brutality and romance, squalour and elegance, corruption and virtue as well as deference and defiance. A time stirring unnoticed changes in the fabric of society which bore revolutionary implications for all social, economic and political life. It was an age which embraced both scientific Determinism and cultural Romanticism and cast up towering figures like Bentham and Carlyle in conflict at the very centre of society.

Into this tension arose Wakley whose prodigious exploits constantly kindled passionate controversy and inflamed the turmoil. Alongside others he shook up his century and affected all our lives. Why is it then that his memory is now eclipsed? In part, I believe, because he was a man of no fixed party which could use his prestige for its own glory. He was what today would be called "his own man". And he remains proof of the inadequacy of Macaulay's dictum that although without party a man may do wonders, he is a mere tongue. Also, his achievements were real and lasting and are now an accepted part of many valued features of our lives that we take for granted. Moreover, it must be acknowledged, many of those who came after him and were beneficiaries of his success found him an embarrassment. For, born into a wealthy family, and retaining the outward trappings of his class, he yet managed to become a prominent advocate not only of medical, social and political reform but also of the deepest aspirations of a working class resolutely excluded from the political arena. Even at the height of Wakley's power and fame G.J. Francis wrote in his *Orators of the Age* in 1847: "If he has not quite conquered the prejudices entertained towards Ultra Radical intruders by men of birth and station he has at least made them feel his intellectual power and acknowledge his moral equality." It is a reasonable assumption that "men of birth and station" have never forgiven him for that or for his political radicalism.

No one attempting this portrait could fail to acknowledge a debt of gratitude to Wakley's official biographer, Sir S. Squire Sprigge, whose book appeared in 1897 to celebrate the centenary of Wakley's birth. Yet, although Sprigge's volume runs to some 500 pages, it is remarkable how many exciting episodes in Wakley's chequered career are completely ignored. The incidents in question are in no way disreputable but they were often highly charged politically and Sprigge frequently took up attitudes to the events and issues which swirled around Wakley at variance with those Wakley himself adopted. Consequently, he might well, as a late Victorian, have considered the omitted items harmful to Wakley's "respectable" memory. Indeed, there must have been an ongoing process since a writer in *The Lancet* of May 19, 1962 admits that: "It took many years after the death of Wakley for the smoke to die down and some of the more dramatic features of his life were in fact not published until the centenary of his birth." So it appears that Sprigge may have taken the lid off some "secrets" but he certainly continued the tradition.

It seems a curious affair today and the omissions my research has uncovered are made good in the present narrative. In fact, Sprigge's partial biography has undoubtedly done harm to Wakley's memory. Even some of those few who know of him and praise his achievements often portray him as having black-and-white vision, of seeing evil everywhere, and of personalizing his fight against injustice. Perhaps they rely too heavily on Dr. Charles Newman's book, *The Evolution of Medical Education in the Nineteenth Century* (1957), which in turn relies upon Sprigge. Newman shows scant regard for

Wakley's reforming zeal, or his personality. Although accepting that Wakley was an extraordinary man he fails to appreciate the irony of a passage about Wakley in George Eliot's *Middlemarch* which he uses to allege that Wakley was hated in his own day, and a "perfect nuisance". So he may have been to some but that is hardly the whole picture. On the contrary, in his own day Wakley's name was a household word among the English people, as his appearance in the novel testifies, and many of them loved him. According to Newman, Wakley enjoyed "... fighting individual people rather than the abuse they represented." As a journalist he is presented as "vulgar and scurrilous in the extreme, a sort of prose Gillray", although Newman does add that he was no worse than many others of the time. And is Gillray such a base example?

Perhaps Newman's own predilections come to the fore when he claims that not for Wakley was inch-by-inch reform, only reform against resistance which produces friction and dissipates energy. "Judged by this standard," he says, "the Wakleys are a mistake; to the romantic who likes disturbances, they are not." It is my opinion that the record shows Wakley had no choice if he was to succeed. But clearly Newman's approach is fundamentally different from Wakley's and is not discernably more suited to the battles in which Wakley was engaged. After all medical and social progress have always depended on healthy tension between radicals and conservatives. And J.F. Clarke, a surgeon who worked on the editorial staff of Wakley's *Lancet* for nearly 40 years, wrote in his *Autobiographical Recollections,* in which he was critical of some of Wakley's actions, "It is doubtful whether if a more scrupulous and righteous course had been pursued, results of such magnitude would have been obtained."

Newman also disparagingly "explains" Wakley's character in terms of an exceedingly feminine spirit residing in a masculine frame. It is also disturbing to find him describing Tom

Duncombe as Wakley's successor as M.P. for Finsbury when he was elected a year prior to Wakley and they sat in the House of Commons as joint representatives of the constituency, and as allies, for 17 years. He further asserts that Wakley's one-time collaborator, David Whittle Harvey, stole papers from a solicitor's office when, in fact, on a charge of having done so he was exonerated by a Select Committee of the House of Commons. As part of his case for reducing Wakley to little more than a mere nuisance, Newman plays down and excuses the scandalous nepotism in the Royal College of Surgeons as well as other abuses Wakley destroyed, by "fighting individuals" and seeking "reforms against resistance".

The truth is that Wakley belongs to that troublesome company of nuisances whose imagination is fired by a sense of social responsibility and who cannot then compromise with complacency. Seeing justice done was for him a public duty rather than a personal conceit. Newman's whole presentation gives an entirely false picture since fuller research reveals that there was a disinterested humanitarian resolve behind all Wakley's diverse activities. He was not a malevolent man in pursuit of a single purpose, but a generous, kind-hearted individual, incapable of bearing malice, who nevertheless refused to underestimate the stakes involved in his varied ventures or the power of his entrenched opponents. To combat evil he saw that he had to attack all its manifestations with all the weapons at his disposal. He was, in the words of J.F. Clarke, involved in events complicated by "passion, prejudice and personal animosity". Such were indeed by-products of momentous conflicts. But he displayed great compassion in his efforts to destroy what he saw as the causes of large-scale suffering, namely poverty and aristocratic dominance. His true claim to fame is as a romantic revolutionary deeply involved in this country's early battles for medical and legal reform, for democracy and for an improved quality of life for the people. As such he can perhaps be better understood today when those struggles have re-emerged with a new content than at the height of Victorian humbug towards the end of the Queen's long reign, or in a period of relative stability.

Wakley's renown and his achievements are due to be resurrected. In my view they cannot fail to excite both the imagination and the admiration of those who find fascination in a past that constantly intrudes into the present.

CHAPTER 1

SURGEONS AND GRAVE-SNATCHERS

In his own day the mere mention of the name Thomas Wakley raised lively passions in the political world and prompted feelings of admiration or panic in the souls of doctors, lawyers, M.P.s, magistrates and the poor. Some were his partisans, other his enemies. Few could ignore him. Engagingly, he was always in scrapes. No words of a biographer can present Wakley as a more colourful and controversial character than he was in real life. But his true significance lies in his influence on the unfolding historical drama of a half-century which contained at first harsh repression and then a Benthamite fervour for far-reaching reform; in fact, the period from the national humiliation of Peterloo, through the fiery emotion of Chartism to the era of mid-century social recovery.

In the early nineteenth century a brilliant but shattering "galaxy of revolutions" was transforming the face of England and English society and generating a vast complex of changes which culminated in the Reform Act of 1832. Subsequent years were to witness a consolidation of the power of the new industrial middle class and the sparking off of the energy and improving spirit of the early Victorian age. One visible manifestation of that spirit was the host of social and legal reformers who sprang up, from whose pioneering work we still benefit today.

Thomas Wakley was one of them. Yet more, he was not only a reformer but a genius in the strategy and tactics of David-and-Goliath struggles, with an unusual capacity to assess and learn from mistakes and failures. His incisive onslaughts on injustice and his unfailing humanity were to win enthusiastic praise from many contemporaries including Sir Robert Peel and Charles

Dickens. Most of the abuses he exposed have long since been swept away. But his involvement in the growth to maturity of the emerging working-class movement and in clashes to achieve vital reform in politics, in medicine and in the cruel and obsolete criminal law, was of considerable influence in the vibrant days of England's impulsion into the modern world.

The village of Membury in Devon, where Wakley was born on July 11, 1795, gave little promise of the improbable future that lay in store for young Thomas. Indeed, strikingly little of his destiny was to be revealed by his childhood and youth. Yet, inevitably they contained the seeds of what was to follow. The times were troubled. In the year Wakley was born, Pitt the Younger was Prime Minister of an England at war with France. Napoleon was threatening to invade and Ireland was in revolt. *Habeas Corpus* had been suspended and the Spithead Mutiny was only two years away. It was also the year that saw the introduction of the Speenhamland system of poor-law relief. Not unnaturally young Thomas in distant Devon was little affected by this menacing background. But the intensified and bitter divisions in the nation that surfaced after the peace and in the subsequent repression interested him deeply, so perhaps the magic was working in his early days, unbeknown to his family or himself. Indeed, he was later to claim proudly that he had felt a great interest in the welfare of the working class from boyhood.

Membury itself has a long history. It boasts a castle, really an Iron Age hill fort, of the kind so well known to Julius Caesar, of which the Old English description was Maen Beorh, "the stone fort". In Saxon times Membury was known grimly as Maimburgh, after the practice of sending there for convalescence soldiers in King Athelstan's armies who were maimed during their victorious but bloody battles with the Danes. In the Domesday Book the village is referred to as part of a manor called Manberia. It will readily be seen how such names could evolve into Membury. At all events its embattled history must have made an impression on Wakley since he gave its name to one of his sons.

Membury today is not a particularly picturesque village. Modern growth has given it a rather sprawling aspect. In Wakley's day it was more compact, but in the centre can still be seen its quaint and narrow main street with the church loftily imposing its grandeur from a rising hillock above. Moreover, it is set in that beautiful countryside of Devon which forms part of a hollow with the rolling hills of Somerset to the north and Dorset to the east. Nearby is the River Yary which flows towards Lyme Regis and Beer, eight miles to the south, where the white cliffs of the coastline begin to turn to red.

The nave of Membury's fine thirteenth-century church, the Church of St. John Baptist, bears tribute to the most illustrious son of the parish with a tactful tablet which reads:

> In Memory
> of
> Thomas Wakley
> Surgeon and Coroner
> Medical and Social
> Reformer
> Member of Parliament
> Founder and First
> Editor of
> The Lancet
> Born at Land Farm
> Membury Devon 1795
> Died in Madeira 1862

This was donated by the proprietors of *The Lancet* and dedicated by the Bishop of Exeter. There is also a plaque at Land Farm.

Wakley's father, Henry (1750-1842), was a wealthy farmer who had inherited the family property including Land Farm. He belonged to the yeoman class which was still very powerful at the time, often rising to the threshold of the peerage and on occasion into it. With his family thus close to the aristocracy, whose monopoly of power was soon to be broken by the rising industrial middle class, it is an irony of fate that young Thomas Wakley was destined to involve himself heart and soul in the social and political struggles of the nascent working class.

Henry Wakley was a man of splendid physique whose active life never faltered until shortly before his death at the age of 92. He also enjoyed his responsibilities. He became one of the leading authorities on agriculture in the West Country and was appointed a Government Commissioner for the Enclosure of Waste Lands.[1] His large family included 11 children, eight sons and three daughters. Of the sons Thomas was the youngest.

All the sons were employed on the farm as soon as they were old enough and, with his brothers, Thomas would be up at sunrise ploughing the fields. The exacting work and the open-air life were elements that helped to produce an all-round sportsman with pride in his great physical strength which was to stand him in good stead throughout his stormy career.

Reluctant Schoolboy

On the other hand Wakley's education was not neglected. For those below the aristocracy boarding schools were virtually unknown at the time. Only later was the full impact of the Industrial Revolution to give rise to a demand for an expanded and improved public school system along the lines pioneered by Dr. Arnold at Rugby, to qualify a new generation of children from the advancing middle class for leadership. Consequently, a local grammar school was considered eminently suitable for the sons of wealthy farmers. Indeed many grammar schools were famous for their teaching and those Wakley was sent to

1.   Appropriation of common wastelands caused considerable displacement and hardship to labourers but at the time many a farmer managed to convince himself that enclosures were desirable for all sections of the community.

were fine examples, light years away from the schools depicted so devastatingly by Dickens.

First he went to Chard, an old centre of radicalism and non-conformity in Somerset. There is no evidence that either of these virtues rubbed off on the young scholar, although his later life suggests that he may well have imbibed something of them. What is known is that he walked to school daily - a journey of six miles in each direction - and that his early education suffered a good deal from bad weather in the winter. The rich valleys of the district, with their fertile loam soil and its subsoil of gravel, became treacherous with snow and swollen streams which made roads impassable and would cut Wakley off from his school for a week or more at a time. Apparently he welcomed these, as well as other, opportunities to playing truant.

Chard School, known as Monmouth House, was built with unusual squared flint enhanced by careful use of ham stone and still stands at the lower end of the town in Fore Street. From its foundation in 1671 the school set the pattern of education in Chard for some two centuries. Its impact on Thomas Wakley is unrecorded, however, and his education there appears from family testimony to have been somewhat intermittent and lacking in lustre. Consequently, he was soon transferred to the even more distinguished grammar school in the ancient town of Honiton, some 10 miles west of Membury. Honiton is well known to travellers as the gateway to Devon, and the vista on approaching it was described by Daniel Defoe in his *Tour Through the Whole Island of Great Britain* as "the most beautiful landskip in the world".

Allhallows Grammar School, as it was known, was founded some time in the sixteenth century and flourished in Honiton until 1938. The building had its origin in the thirteenth century and it is not only by far the oldest in the town but predates Exeter Cathedral and many other famous Devon churches and houses. A rose window in the west wall bears the date 1614, which is when a John Fley left his lands in trust to help the education of poor boys at the school and assist them to go to university. The building, with its rose window, still stands and the cold-stone classrooms in which young Thomas Wakley pursued his lessons now fittingly house the Honiton Museum.

When Wakley took his lessons at Allhallows the headmaster was the Reverend Richard Lewis who guided the school for no less than 42 years from 1801-1843. No register or other document of Wakley's time exists but he was a near contemporary of the future Sir Alfred Stephen, G.C.M.G. Stephen was at the school from 1811 to 1815. Later, he became a Judge, rising to be Chief Justice of the Supreme Court of New South Wales, Lieutenant Governor of that Province, and a Privy Councillor. He died in Sydney, Australia, on October 15, 1894, at the great age of 92.

Stephen recorded some impressions of his old school, and the high regard in which Lewis was held by his former pupil is clearly indicated in the following extracts from a letter written by him in 1886:

> And of our good master and his wife, Dr. and Mrs. Lewis, I think invariably with great regard. Whatever I have exhibited in my career of precision, in thought or writing, a quality without which no man can achieve success on the Bench or at the Bar, I owe to the vigour with which Lewis insisted on it, in construing, in composition, and on accuracy in prosody as well as grammar.

Wakley too must have benefited from the regime of Lewis since, without going on to university, his adult career was to reveal extensive knowledge and learning as well as a brilliant ability to make the most of this asset.

It was whilst a schoolboy at Allhallows at the age of eight that the restless Thomas became anxious to go to sea. This arose from his passion for walking which often took him to the bay of Lyme Regis which was clearly visible from the top of Membury Castle, and to Beer, then a small fishing village with lofty chalk cliffs and tales of illicit smuggling. Two years later his dream came true when his father reluctantly agreed to his joining a voyage to Calcutta in an East Indiaman. Thus he became Midshipman Wakley, aged 10. His father's hesitation was allayed by the captain, who was a personal friend, agreeing to take the young man under his care.

However, experiences on the voyage destroyed his craving for a sea-faring life when the captain died on the return passage. The remainder of the journey appears to have been unpleasant to say the least. Wakley returned without his sea chest and bitterly complained of the severe hardships he had encountered. He declined to expand upon his torments and what they were we may never know. But his self-imposed silence provides a clue. Brutality at sea was rife at the time and the agony and injury caused by keelhauling, for example, give a clear illustration of the depths to which it could go. In the absence of a protective captain the young boy may also have suffered assault and indecent abuse from thugs among the crew. Such distressing ill-treatment might well account for his later efforts to assist the underdog and his becoming an improbable Radical. After all, his wealthy family background and his harsh experiences of life below decks demonstrated two opposing traditions whose interplay must have influenced him when the time came consciously to choose between them.

Guy's Hospital

In the meantime, after an interval in which to settle down, Wakley returned to normal education, possibly at Wellington

Grammar School near Taunton but not Wiveliscombe, as cited by Sprigge and Brook, since it had no Grammar School. There he remained until he chose medicine as a career and was apprenticed to an apothecary at Taunton. This choice of career led to a significant turn in his life. For the medical profession presented an unsavoury image which Wakley was to learn to detest. Like the other ancient professions medicine was then very different from what it is today. There was no medical register and medical ethics were neither practised nor even recognized by the great majority of the profession. Indeed it is difficult to comprehend today that many practitioners received no professional education, and possessed no medical qualifications, of any kind. In consequence ignorant quacks frequently got away with murder from knowing too little or wrongly using knowledge that could become dangerous.

The qualified limb of the profession, such as it was, was split three ways between physicians, surgeons and apothecaries. The physicians were pre-eminent in the social hierarchy and were regarded as gentry. They were required to have obtained a university degree in classics and to be members of the Royal College of Physicians. They also purported to observe a strict ethical code founded on the oath of Hippocrates - a claim vigorously challenged by Wakley.

The surgeons, wanting to climb the social ladder, had broken away from the company of Barber-Surgeons in 1745 but to their chagrin were still regarded as inferior. Without anaesthesia surgery was an unsavoury and bloody affair, unattractive to many persons of sensibility. Moreover, even here there was no established course of professional education and no legal requirement to be qualified. Nevertheless, in 1800 the Royal College of Surgeons had been transformed from a City livery company into a chartered corporation, although it was only later, after Wakley's devastating onslaughts on it, that it introduced more demanding requirements for qualification. By the time Wakley was a medical student the formal basis of the surgeon's training was meant to be a combination of apprenticeship with courses in anatomy and surgery and what was known as "walking the wards". The reality, however, was often quite different.

The apothecaries, who had separated from the grocers as early as 1617, were the third and, in public perception, the lowest grade of the medical profession. They were the general practitioners and also chemists, since they were allowed by law to keep an open shop. Like surgeons they had to start by way of apprenticeship but they had also to pass examinations in chemistry, anatomy and medicine. By an Act of 1815 they were granted a virtual monopoly in the dispensing of medicines.

Physicians and surgeons had the greatest contempt for apothecaries, regarding them as shopkeepers; after all they sold drugs like tradesmen. This gave them an incentive to sell as many as possible which undoubtedly offended slowly developing notions of professional ethics. Perhaps because of that the despised apothecaries were the first professional body to establish a system of qualification and registration which the physicians and surgeons were later compelled to emulate.

It was against this background that young Wakley entered upon his apprenticeship to the apothecary. However, with a farming background he was not too sensitive to blood, and with the enthusiasm of youth he was ambitious to become a leading surgeon. He persuaded his father, therefore, to allow him to leave the apothecary to become a pupil of his brother-in-law, Mr. Phelps, a surgeon at Beominster. Later he joined, as an assistant, another surgeon and in 1815 at the age of 20, he travelled to London to complete his studies. Two years later, he obtained his surgeon's diploma at the United Hospitals of St. Thomas's and Guy's. Here too he was to tread the path that led to violent conflict with authority and to fame.

The appalling conditions of life in the slum areas south of

London Bridge at the time are well known from the works of Dickens, particularly Oliver Twist. In such uncongenial surroundings the unsophisticated, country-bred Wakley found lodgings off Tooley Street in order to be near the United Hospitals. St. Thomas's then occupied a large site fronting Guy's on which London Bridge Station now stands. It boasted two large squares and its church was later to become the Chapter House of Southwark Cathedral. Anatomy classes were held only at St. Thomas's but the students, if they were sufficiently motivated, attended surgical practice and operations at both institutions.

When Wakley was a student, Sir Astley Paston Cooper, Bart. (1768-1841) was an overwhelming personality at the United Hospitals. Although his father was a well-to-do clergyman Astley Cooper's boyhood was more turbulent than Wakley's. There is, in fact, a hint of desperation in the way he was finally packed off as a pupil to his uncle, a London surgeon. However, he quickly rose to eminence, affluence and the head of his profession. At 21 he became demonstrator of anatomy at St. Thomas's and in 1800, after a prudent change of political opinions, he was elected surgeon to Guy's Hospital; two years later he became a Fellow of the Royal Society. He married an heiress and by 1815, with the Prince Regent among his patients, he had, for the time, the enormous annual income of £21,000. His influence was immense and at the hospitals he wielded unchallenged power.

By contrast, Wakley as a student was something of a puritan. Not for him the coarse life of most medical students with their over-indulgence in ale, black tobacco and Fleet Street brothels. Still, he was a very energetic and hearty young man, popular with his fellow students and renowned among them for his physical strength and powers of endurance. Although an industrious student he also found time to become a keen cricketer, a skilful billiards player and an exceptionally fine boxer. It was a feature of the day that many public houses, like later fairgrounds, employed a pugilist to entertain the customers by putting on the gloves and taking on all-comers. Wakley was frequently to be seen accepting the challenge with great skill and success.

In 1815 young Wakley received from his father an allowance of £80 a year. This sum had to cover his hospital and tuition fees of £20, board and lodging, clothing and pocket money. He shared a room with a friend at a weekly rent of eight shillings and went out for his meals to ordinaries, which provided set meals at fixed prices, and taverns where he would spend two shillings or so a day. Nothing was left for travelling expenses and for his annual holiday he used to walk to his Devonshire home. A truly impressive feat but not surprising given his enthusiasm for walking.

Whilst a student, Wakley attended three courses of instruction in anatomy, was present at Sir Astley Cooper's lectures on the Practice of Surgery and obtained some experience of surgical dressing in the wards. Facilities for dissecting were curtailed, however, owing to the dearth of bodies which were then obtainable from only two sources. The legitimate source - although restricted and often intercepted by relatives - was the gallows.

Agents of the surgeons were usually conspicuous on hanging days. And because the surgeons wanted the bodies in order to advance the cause of scientific medicine they were aided by government which made the trade legal for its own less praiseworthy reasons. In fact, The Murder Act (1752) quite openly declared: "It is become necessary that some further Terror and peculiar Mark of Infamy be added to the Punishment." Death followed by mutilation was seen as a form of aggravated capital punishment, intended, as a general deterrent, to intimidate the common people. Only the bodies of executed murderers, therefore, could lawfully be used for dissection.

However, to some extent this policy had the opposite effect from that intended. Relatives and friends of felons about to hang would travel vast distances and engage in both spectacular and ingenious activities to prevent corpses falling into the hands of the surgeons. Stories abound of relatives and surgeons' agents chasing each other's carts through the narrow streets of London to recover or steal corpses. Sometimes surgeons' agents even masqueraded as parents or other relatives of the dead to secure the bodies without the use of force, which at other times they would use without hesitation. And, of course, not least concerned were those condemned to death who frequently appealed to their close ones to ensure they received a burial in one piece.

As John Gay observed in *The Beggar's Opera:* "Poor Brother Tom had an accident this time Twelvemonth, and so clever a made fellow he was, that I could not save him from those fleaing Rascals the Surgeons; and now poor man, he is among the Otamys at Surgeons Hall." Without doubt fear of mutilation, with mystic overtones, was often greater than the fear of death.

The illegitimate source of corpses was the "resurrection man". The number of persons executed in the whole of England and Wales from 1805 to 1820 was 1,150. Not all reached the dissecting table whereas the average number of students entering the London medical schools alone was estimated at nearly a thousand a year, and the number of bodies required at least two thousand a year. As practical anatomy could only be learned by dissection body-snatching from graveyards was considered by the medical profession a necessary evil. Even so it was insufficient and as late as December 10, 1831, all the members of the Council of the Royal College of Surgeons were to sign a Memorial to Lord Melbourne, the Home Secretary, pointing to the difficulties of procuring a supply of bodies for anatomical purposes and asking that Parliament find a solution. The Memorial was presented to the House of Commons on Saturday, December 17 where a campaign by Wakley led to the rejection of the Anatomy Bill which sought to legalize the sale of bodies - a sure temptation to murder. Needless to say it did nothing to improve the surgeon's image in the eyes of the public.

In fact, body-snatching became not only a ghoulish occupation but also a flourishing minor industry. Its practitioners were both swift and skilful and they affected the pride of craftsmen. Bold and impudent they charged monopoly prices and frequently were not above blackmail. Scarcely a trace of their actions was left in the graveyards. Indeed it was easy enough to bribe sextons and others who looked after cemeteries and for most it was not necessary to follow the murderous example of the notorious Burke and Hare in Edinburgh and Bishop and Williams in London, in providing their own "subjects".[2] Just how serious the problem was is revealed by Sir Astley Cooper who went so far as to tell a Select Committee: "The law does not prevent our obtaining the body of an individual if we think proper; for there is no person, let his situation in life be what it may, whom, if I were disposed to dissect, I could not obtain ... nobody is secured by the law; it only adds to the price of the subject."

Of course, any outrage can be pointed up by treating it humorously and an outstanding example, using the body-snatcher's grim trade, is to be found in the closing stanzas of Thomas Hood's comic poem, *Mary's Ghost, a Pathetic Ballad.* The ghost explains that her grave has been rifled and the contents distributed among the anatomical teachers of London in the following words:

2.   With a sense of rough justice, when Bishop and Williams were executed their bodies were handed over for dissection by order of the Judge.

The arm that used to take your arm is took to Dr. Vyse.
And both my legs are gone to walk the Hospital at Guy's.

I vowed that you should have my hand but Fate gives us denial;
You'll find it there at Mr. Bell's in spirits in a phial.

As for my feet, the little feet you used to call so pretty,
There's one I know in Bedford Row, the t' other's in the City.

I can't tell where my head has gone, but Dr. Carpue can;
As for my trunk it's all packed up to go by Pickford's van.

I wish you'd go to Mr. P. And save me such a ride. I don't half
like the outside place they've took for my inside.

The cock it crows, I must be gone, my William we must part:
And I'll be yours in death although Sir Astley has my heart.

As the resurrection men grew more skilled and perhaps faced greater risks, their fees increased. A professor of anatomy at a hospital would pay £10 for a body and the owner of a private school even more. A student had to pay upwards of £2 for a limb. John Hunter, under whom Sir Astley Cooper had studied, even went so far as to pay £500 in bribes for the body of the much publicized giant O'Byrne. The body-snatcher could usually get his price since there was a seller's market, and if his demands were not met he would often deposit decomposing parts of a body near to the entrance of a medical school.

Whilst this unsavoury traffic in corpses proceeded Wakley was able to take two important courses in practical anatomy and in October 1817 he qualified for membership of the Royal College of Surgeons. The ordeal of the examination he characterized as "the veriest farce imaginable". He then walked to Membury to inform his family of the good news. Some 16 years later, as we shall see, he was to play his part in destroying the grave-snatching trade with the Anatomy Act of 1832. This permitted only the use of "unclaimed" workhouse bodies and solely in schools of anatomy licensed under the Act. Even then an inspector had to certify the circumstances of death.

CHAPTER 2

"ATROCIOUS ATTEMPT TO MURDER"

One thing is clear, Wakley acquired more than medical knowledge from his experiences as a student. He was quick to express indignation at what he rapidly perceived to be unfair treatment of students. For example, presence at the crucially important post-mortem examinations could be obtained only by tipping the porters. Again, only the favoured pupils of the surgeons were notified when operations were to be performed and the teaching staff often failed to visit their students, or gave precious little help when they did. Above all, if, as with Wakley, a pupil could not pay exorbitant fees to a "great man" he became a second-class student or less. According to Sir Astley Cooper, a student aiming high also had to be able to afford to study at Edinburgh or on the Continent. He managed to do both.

Despite his anger, at this time Wakley was not intent on a career of reform. His only desire was to practice as a G.P. in his native Devon. However, after months of trying he could find no suitable opportunity and felt he had no alternative but to return to London and enter private practice in the City. Here he took up residence and continued to study in Gerard's Hall, an old inn which before the Great Fire had been the palace of the Lord Mayors of London. Gerard's Hall stood in Basing Lane and was later cleared in the construction of the present Queen Victoria Street.

For a time fortune seemed to favour the young surgeon. A wealthy lead merchant named Joseph Goodchild had warehouses and offices in Tooley Street, near St. Thomas's Hospital, where he employed between 200 and 300 "hands". Many of these men were frequently in need of the services of the hospital and some received surgical assistance daily.

Joseph Goodchild, no doubt for good business reasons, was a governor of St. Thomas's and an annual subscriber to its funds. Nevertheless, such payments did not match what his income would allow or what the charity hospital expected in the light of his constant use of its services.

Accordingly, Wakley and a friend, while still students, found themselves calling upon Mr. Goodchild at his opulent home in Hendon, then a distant rural village, to see if he might be prevailed upon to make a larger-than-usual subscription to the hospital following the issue of a special appeal by its treasurer. The young men must have made a favourable impression on Mr. Goodchild for he handed over £100 and invited them first to lunch and later to a party at his house. Here they were introduced to two of their host's daughters. This in turn quickly led, after ardent courtships, to two engagements, both of which received Goodchild's blessing. With Wakley this was somewhat remarkable for the time since he was a younger son, unlikely ever to inherit Land Farm.

Goodchild continued, however, to treat his future son-in-law with lavish generosity and gave Wakley the capital required to acquire not only the lease of a large house in fashionable Argyll Street, off Regent Street, but also princely furnishing for the house and the goodwill of a successful practice. The nearby town house of the Earl of Aberdeen gave an aristocratic touch to Argyll Street and Wakley's house itself boasted 15 rooms including a double dining room, a large drawing room, half-a-dozen bedrooms and a rear study which was used as a surgery. At first the venture was a great success. But fate soon intervened with shattering effect.

It has been suggested by John Stanhope in his book *The Cato Street Conspiracy* (1962) that Joseph Goodchild insisted, as a condition of his generous support of Wakley and his consent to his daughter's engagement, that Wakley establish a West End practice with a rich clientele. That is no doubt true.

But Stanhope's conclusion that Wakley's love for Miss Goodchild was stronger than his social conscience, that he put aside his inclination to plunge into radicalism and reform and that his wings were clipped by Goodchild seem wide of the mark. Wakley undoubtedly had developed a social conscience, probably from influences already mentioned, but there is no evidence of a tendency to radicalism at this time. On the contrary, as we shall see, there is a good deal to indicate that such an inclination was not stirred until a little later.

In any event, on February 5, 1820 Thomas Wakley was duly married to Elizabeth, the youngest Miss Goodchild, at the fashionable St. James's Church in Piccadilly. The report of his wedding in the newspapers of the following day coincided with the news of the death of King George III. The marriage was one of love and affection and Wakley's professional prospects had become extremely promising. Young, talented, handsome and healthy he was admired by his friends and respected by his patients. Yet, in six months his home was broken up, his house burnt to the ground, his health impaired, his practice destroyed and his reputation tarnished. The causes of the tragedy, from which he was young and resourceful enough to recover, are only now becoming fully understood. Such attacks were commonplace enough in the West End of London when it had no effective policing. But this had more than enough ingredients to suggest something other than a spontaneous assault and theft.

What is transparently clear is that on the evening of August 26, 1820 Wakley was murderously assaulted by a mysterious gang of men. The *Morning Chronicle* of Monday, August 28, reported in detail the extraordinary events of that night. It is worth repeating at length for its intrinsic interest and also to compare with testimony given in the High Court action which followed.

ATROCIOUS ATTEMPT TO MURDER, SUPPOSED ROBBERY, AND SETTING A HOUSE ON FIRE.

Yesterday morning, about half-past one o'clock a man called at the house of Mr. Wakley, surgeon, of No. 5 Argyll Street, Oxford Street, and knocked at the door. All the servants were in bed, and Mr. W., who was indisposed, was in his apartment putting some leeches to his temples. He placed a bandage round his head and proceeded to open the door, on doing which, a man, who appeared to be flurried, said that he had come from Mr. Ibbetson, of the Bath Hotel, Basing Lane, an old patient of Mr. Wakley's, who was dangerously ill, and required his immediate attendance. The fellow requesting a glass of cyder, as he said he was fatigued by a long journey, Mr. Wakley complied and went downstairs to the cellar to procure him a glass. During this time it is supposed that the villain admitted some accomplices. On the Doctor's return to the passage he observed something rush towards him, and at the moment he received a tremendous blow on the head which knocked him down. It was with some instrument, and at the same time the destructive weapon of the assassin was aimed at his breast, on which he received a stab; he then thrust the instrument a second time, which passed through the collar of the Doctor's coat, waistcoat, and neckcloth, and penetrated the skin; he received other injuries, and while he lay in the passage he received violent blows and kicks from some person or persons; his abdomen was severely bruised. In this deplorable state he lay for three-quarters of an hour without the least assistance, when he was roused from his stupor by the flames in immense bodies rushing down the stairs and a dense smoke. He with difficulty arose and crawled out the back way, and climbed through the skylight leading to the house of Mr. Thompson, next door, in whose parlour he was afterwards found weltering in his blood and apparently in a dying state. He was immediately carried to the house of Mr. Parker, of Argyll Street, where Drs. Luke and Cates attended and dressed his wounds. On Mr. Wakley being supported to the above house a daring villain unfeelingly snatched at his watch and got it from his fob. He had the presence of mind to seize the villain by the collar; the property was recovered and he was taken in

Dr. Thomas Wakley, M.P.
Reproduced by kind permission of the TUC Library

Chard School, Somerset

Chard School, Somerset

The rose window with the wording "All Hallows Grammar School"

custody to the watch-house. Mr. W., after being dressed, was put to bed, and yesterday morning he bled himself; and fearful that his wife, to whom he was lately married, should be alarmed by the too speedy intelligence of the atrocious deed, although in so dreadful a condition, proceeded to his country residence yesterday morning. Three-quarters of an hour elapsed before the fire was discovered by Mr. W., who, as well as he was able, gave an alarm; the servants immediately arose and made their escape. A lamplighter broke the windows of the parlour, on which the flames burst forth in a great body and the neighbourhood was in a moment illumined. The utmost confusion prevailed, and the inmates of the adjacent houses were seen, in almost a condition of nudity, taking refuge in other houses.

In a short time several engines arrived, and, having plenty of water, played with great activity on the element which seemed to threaten destruction to all around it, and persons employed in saving the furniture. In a few hours the house of Mr. Wakley was gutted, and what property there was in the house - if not stolen - was destroyed. Property consisting of guineas to an immense amount were in one of the upper apartments, and the firemen will be employed to search in order to ascertain if any robbery was committed, or if the above transaction proceeded from malice.

The mysterious affair has caused many suspicions. A short time ago Mr. Wakley received several threatening letters, signed "Jealousy is the cause, but it is from a friend." The man who called is unknown to Mr. Wakley, and the case is involved in great mystery. During the course of the day various persons of distinction about the neighbourhood made inquiry after the state of Mr. Wakley, and the answer was "Although severely injured there are hopes of his recovery" ...

The surgeons who examined the wounds on the body of Mr. Wakley did not think that they were of so serious a nature as to affect his life, the fortunate circumstances of his having put the bandage about his head prior to opening the door prevented the violent blow he received having a serious effect. The blow was given with some heavy instrument, and must have been given with some deadly intention ...

Widespread interest and curiosity were aroused by the story. Why, it was asked, was a recently qualified and newly wed surgeon so brutally attacked with intent to murder? His attackers, excluding the watch-thief who was presumably a bystander, were never traced but it was generally assumed that they were uncaptured participants in the Cato Street Conspiracy. The reason is not far to seek. According to a contemporary booklet it was widely rumoured that Wakley was the masked man in the disguise of a sailor who decapitated the dead bodies of Arthur Thistlewood and his fellow conspirators after their execution on May 1, 1820. The booklet *Facts relative to the Late Fire and Attempt to Murder Mr. Wakley* was written in 1820 by William Gardiner, the master of a dancing school known as the Lydney Academy and a friend of Wakley, who obtained and published statements from all the witnesses to the assault and arson.

The Cato Street Conspiracy

To consider the rumours more fully it is of interest to take a look at the Cato Street Plot itself. On the dark night of February 23, 1820, acting on "information received" a group of Bow Street Runners and soldiers raided a dilapidated room above a disused stable still standing today in Cato Street, a back street parallel to the Edgware Road. Here they surprised a party of poor but spirited men handling a quantity of arms. In the ensuing scuffle one of the Bow Street officers was run through with a sword and killed.

The men may have been Spencean Philanthropists, followers of Thomas Spence, a recently deceased bookseller who in the years of distress and repression in the aftermath of the French Revolution and the Napoleonic Wars believed power could only be won for the downtrodden by means of violence. On the other hand there is evidence to show that the majority of them were close to starvation and were merely seeking the means to live. This would not apply to their leader Thistlewood, however, since he was highly political and articulate. Indeed, he had already been deeply implicated in the Spa Field Riots of 1816, notwithstanding his acquittal at his subsequent trial for high treason.

After some, but by no means all, of the Cato Street conspirators had been arrested a government statement was issued claiming that there had been a diabolical plot to start a revolution by assassinating the entire Cabinet at one of their periodical dinners. This completely ignored the fact that such dinners had been discontinued as a mark of respect for George III who, as we have seen, had died earlier the same month. The signal for the general revolt, it was proclaimed, was to be the parading of Castlereagh's head on a pike and the posting of notices declaring that a Provisional Government was sitting and calling on all friends of Liberty and the People to come forward. Preliminary bills had, in fact, already been posted by government agents and were thought to be genuine by both public and police. For trying to prevent the destruction of one in Glasgow Mr. Andrew Hardie, a perfectly law-abiding radical ancestor of Keir Hardie, was executed in an atrocious use of the harsh criminal law of the time.

The conspirators were soon charged with high treason and brought to trial before a Special Commission at the Old Bailey in April 1820. The evidence of Robert Adams, an accused who turned King's evidence, was deemed conclusive as to both the plot and the killing of a police officer by Thistlewood who was not permitted to produce witnesses. The men's solicitor, who acted without fee, was the experienced Alderman Harmer whose name was well known to readers of the Newgate Calender in consequence of having represented numerous prisoners in famous trials at the Old Bailey. He briefed as counsel John Adolphus who, like so many others, we shall meet in conflict with Wakley later. It was a wise choice for although Adolphus had no sympathy with the conspirators' aims he defended them with vigour, skill and courage. He strenuously attempted to secure the production for cross-examination of one George Edwards, but to no avail. Despite Edwards being first an accused and then appearing on the Crown list of witnesses for the prosecution he had been secreted away and was too well hidden by the Home Secretary, Lord Sidmouth, to be found. Although Sidmouth was often portrayed at the time as being the most honourable of men, the poet Shelley presented the more general assessment when he penned his famous lines:

> I met Murder on the way - He had a mask like Castlereagh.
> Very smooth he looked, yet grim, seven blood-hounds followed him.

> Clothed with the Bible, as with light and the shadows of the night
> Like Sidmouth, next, Hypocrisy, on a crocodile rode by.

Thistlewood alleged that the whole plot was the invention of Edwards who was, in truth, later revealed to be a government spy. It was indeed proved at the trial that all the weapons had been made at Edwards' order, to Edwards' design and paid for with his money although previously he had never been able to find the price of a pint of beer. It was established too that not only did the Cabinet not meet at dinner on the night in question but that a special notice of a fictitious "grand Cabinet dinner" had been planted in one of the newspapers and "discovered" by none other than Edwards. In fact, it had been known to Ministers at least two months before February 23, that there was a plot afoot to assassinate them. So they secretly hatched a plan to direct and then "uncover" it. Thistlewood never denied the scheme[1] and, in his final plea from the dock, he openly stated that he was actuated by concern for the welfare of his

---

1.   Although he claimed to have turned down Edwards' plans to blow up the House of Commons and attack Ministers at a fete to be given by the Spanish Ambassador on the grounds that he wished to punish the guilty only. Like Cicero he believed tyrranicide justified.

starving countrymen and indignation at the massacre at Peterloo. He had resolved, he added, "that the lives of the instigators should be the requiem to the souls of the murdered innocents ..."

The plot never had the remotest chance of success but its disclosure created the sensation the government required in its eager attempts to discredit the more responsible reform movement and its leaders whom the government greatly feared. It was a sequel to Sidmouth's notorious, repressive Six Acts and was used to justify them. In the event, however, a combination of the general distress and disaffection in the country, the feebleness and fantasy-ridden nature of the conspiracy and the unsavoury role of Edwards as an *agent provocateur* produced widespread sympathy for the men who were executed. Thistlewood, in particular, was the focus of much support. On the day following his trial *The Times* published an account of the proceedings in a special supplement the same size as the paper itself. However, when Thistlewood came to make his last speech from the dock he vigorously attacked the Judges and the injustice of the trial in best radical tradition and unnerved *The Times* into calling for the full penalty against him whatever the law might think right for the others.

Edwards, meanwhile, had been spirited away to Guernsey from where he wrote a number of pathetic letters to Henry Hobhouse, Under-Secretary at the Home Office, which can now be read in Home Office file 44/6 at the Public Record Office. He wanted more money and his family with him. More important, he was seriously obsessed with being recognized and hated the venom his name evoked even in the island of his exile. "Everyone," he whined, "Seems to Rail against Me (instead of which I anticipated praise from all)." He learned that Thistlewood's widow Susan, who was denied her husband's body for burial and even a lock of his hair, had sworn a Bill of

Indictment against him for high treason. Susan was a Jacobin in her own right and her determination to bring Edwards to justice if she could frightened the life out of him. He also seemed to have some fears that the government might disown him although they could hardly have done so. He pleaded persistently with Hobhouse to have him settled elsewhere with his family, preferably the Cape of Good Hope. What finally happened to him is not recorded but his letters show beyond doubt that the lot of an *agent provocateur* is not always a happy one. He may even have been disposed of by Sidmouth's men.

He and his masters certainly aroused bitter anger. Sidmouth, and others, received numerous threats of assassination unless they brought Edwards to justice whilst Thistlewood was sent letters in gaol praising him as a martyr and assuring him that his aims would still be achieved. One letter sent to Sidmouth, dated April 13, 1820 and written in a good round hand, was addressed to "Ministers, Privy Councillors, Bloody Minded Wretches." It continues, "Ye are now brooding with hellish delight on the sacrifice you intend to make of those poor creatures ye took out of Cato St. on pretence of punishing them for what your own horrid spies and agents instigated and found them the means of doing." After claiming the government was filling the streets with soldiers and cannon to murder the people as "your beloved friend Ferdinand" had done in Spain the writer continues, "But know this ye demons - on an approaching day and in an hour when you least expect it shall ye yourselves fall in sacrifice to the just vengeance of an oppressed and suffering people who shall behold your bloody corpses dragged in triumph through their streets."

Within three days of being condemned to death the men were sent to the gallows outside Newgate prison on May Day 1820 in the presence of an enormous crowd which had to be held in check by two troops of the Life Guards. Thistlewood asked the crowd to remember he died in the cause of liberty and people hissed, groaned and cried out "murder, murder, murder". The bodies were allowed to hang for half an hour after which they were taken down and placed face up in coffins with their heads over the end. Then a masked man dressed as a seaman stepped forward to decapitate them. So deftly and quickly did he perform the gruesome task that many of the spectators suspected that he was a member of the medical profession. Indeed, *The Times* wrote: "... he seemed to be a young man. His mode of operation showed evidently that he was a surgeon" (May 2, 1820). The crowd grew increasingly ugly and vociferously gave vent to their feelings of disgust towards the unknown man in the mask. Soon similar sentiments were widely echoed throughout the land.

Another newspaper article gave credence to the widespread rumours by asserting that the masked "sailor" was a young surgeon who, it gratuitously added, practised in Argyll Street. No one at the time seems to have asked why such a specific assertion should be made or who originally gave voice to it. As a result the truth cannot now be known. However, as Thomas Wakley was the only surgeon in Argyll Street suspicion naturally fell upon him, as was presumably intended by someone. It is a strange episode since there is no evidence of Wakley having any bitter enemies at this time of his life.

As at least 20 of the Cato Street conspirators had escaped and were still at large it was widely believed that the attempt on Wakley's life was an act of revenge on their part for the mutilation of their comrades. Certainly Wakley himself thought so. Yet it has never been proved, and it must be remembered that Wakley had received, both before and after his marriage, anonymous threatening letters inspired by jealousy. So perhaps he had aroused hatred in at least one person after all.

Indeed, some of his family believed a disappointed suitor of Elizabeth wrote the threatening letters and was implicated in the assault and arson.

One such letter, which was received in March 1820, well before the execution of Thistlewood, actually threatened that his house would be burnt down and he himself murdered. He took the threat seriously enough to consult his solicitors and on their advice doubled the insurance on the contents of his house to £1,200; the additional £600 to cover goods bought since he had taken out the insurance prior to his marriage. Unfortunately, in the event, he delayed doing so until shortly before the fire.

As a consequence of this letter no credence was given to the theory that the attack was the work of Thistlewood's friends by Wakley's early biographer Sir S.S. Sprigge. However, evidence in Home Office records confirms the existence of men who were determined to avenge the beheadings. It reads as follows:

Thomas Davies and Henry Gascoigne were attacked in Mare Pond, an obscure street near St. Thomas's Hospital in consequence of the former having been reported as the person who beheaded Thistlewood and his following. The error arose from the former young gentleman having taken a head from St. Thomas's to dissect at his lodgings and it was consequently reported he was the executioner.

They were beat most dreadfully and it will be months before they can leave their lodgings, as the villains attempted to cut off their testicles.

Hospital surgeons have subscribed 15 guineas.

The mystery will probably now never be solved but Wakley's own view as to who the perpetrators of the outrage were is clearly entirely credible. And he was determined not to allow the identity of the man in the mask to remain shrouded in secrecy. He wrote to the Sheriff of London, J.W. Perkins, to request an official denial of "this disgusting falsehood". The Sheriff replied that the whole

> ... disgusting business was conducted with such privacy and pertinacious concealment from me that I was not even made acquainted with the order for the execution until the day after it had been determined upon ... As to the man who decapitated Thistlewood and his companions, he was procured for that purpose by the prison surgeon, and his terms £20 agreed for by Mr. Turner ... In answer to my inquiry the other day (in consequence of your note) who the fellow was, Mr. Turner informed me that he was a resurrection man who obtained bodies for the hospitals, and that when he asked him if he could perform the task of cutting off the heads, he replied, "oh, yes, that he could do it very well, as he was in the habit of cutting off *nobs* [heads] for the purpose of obtaining *nackers* [teeth]."

The publication of the Sheriff's letter swiftly cleared Wakley's name but did nothing to expose the true identity of the resurrectionist. He was, almost certainly, a hospital porter named Tom Parker, a celebrated grave-robber who boasted that he once took 14 bodies out of old St. Pancras churchyard in a single night. He subsequently became assistant to William Adams, F.R.C.S., Curator of the Museum and Demonstrator of Morbid Anatomy at St. Thomas's Hospital. Many years later Adams was to give an interesting account of the style of Tom Parker and the hazards of meeting death near St. Thomas's.

> In 1843 I found that the museum was very short of separated bones of the skull, and I asked Tom to look out for any favourable opportunities. A young woman about 18 years of age threw herself over Waterloo Bridge and died at the hospital. Tom said her head was just the thing I wanted, and, when we were alone after the post-mortem, he said: "Now I

should like to show you the secret of cutting off a head." The knife, he said, would never do it, but there was a dodge in wrenching through the ligaments by twisting the head violently first to the right and then to the left after all the soft parts had been cut through. This he demonstrated on the spot by putting the girl on the floor, then raising the trunk and firmly grasping it between his knees, when he made the cut in front, sloping the knife towards the occipital articulation and then the cut behind with the same slope in the knife. Then the violent wrench and the head came off. Tom was generally accused of being the man on the scaffold, and never denied it, but he never confessed it even to myself, next to Grainger his best friend.

The sequel to Tom Parker's case of decapitation was remarkable. The coroner's jury returned a verdict of felo-de-se, and the woman was buried in unconsecrated ground close to the churchyard of St. Thomas's Hospital. The beadle of the parish and a few others were at the grave and the beadle said his duty was to see that the body was in the coffin. This, of course, Tom Parker resisted, and a few others that were at the grave; but the beadle got his pickaxe and forced open the coffin, when it was found that there was no head. Then the people adjourned to the public-house close by and Tom ran off to the hospital, put the head on with a little sawdust over the neck. Tom Parker then went down to the public-house and faced the mob. Tom made a speech and said: "'Now this 'ere beadle says the woman was brought from St. Thomas's Hospital without her head. Now I mean to say that the beadle is drunk, and I insist that all the people here come to the grave and see for themselves." Away the crowd went, and the woman, sure enough, had a head on, and he turned the tables on the beadle.

Despite what he says here about Parker's failure to confess Adams did identify him as the man who cut off the heads of the Cato Street conspirators. Apparently he wished to exonerate a friend upon whom suspicion of being the man in the mask had fallen after Wakley had been cleared. For that reason a weak doubt must still survive.

Imputed Lucifer

To return to the sequel to the fire, Wakley's insurers, the Hope Fire Assurance Company, refused his claim. They simply alleged that he had destroyed his own house. Why they did so in the face of the testimony of all the eye-witnesses collected by William Gardiner and of Wakley's serious injuries can only be conjectured. Presumably they were suspicious of Wakley increasing his cover shortly before the fire. But it would be astonishing if they were not informed of the letter threat and his solicitor's advice.

Wakley's own affidavit on the events was similar to the report contained in the *Morning Chronicle.* His next-door neighbour, Samuel Parker, in his deposition pointed out that:

Mr. Wakley was in a most dreadful state; his senses were obviously deranged, and the horror and dread he exhibited, imagining all around him to be the murderers, were excessive. He had shiverings, or rather tremblings, apparently the effect of mental horror, as they were accompanied with the gestures and clenching of his hands which caused me to hold him firmly, lest I should suffer violence; a profuse perspiration covered his face and he showed symptoms of great agony. His hand, face, shirt, and cravat were much covered with blood and dirt, and the blood gushed from his left ear and trickled down his neck. One of

Mr. Thompson's servants brought some water, which he drank greedily, and with great difficulty I restrained him from drinking of it too copiously.

In what was probably his first brush with the law, but certainly not his last, Wakley sued the insurance company confident in the forensic strength of the evidence which would be given in his support. The case was heard in the King's Bench before the Lord Chief Justice Abbott and a jury, on June 21, 1821. Thomas Denman, a legal reformer and subsequent Lord Chief Justice, appeared for Wakley with John Adolphus as his junior. Opening the case he emphasized that the plaintiff was a young man with a wealthy father-in-law, and that there was no justification for supposing that he was in need of ready money. Certainly, there was no motive for him to set fire to his own house. Furthermore, not all his losses were covered by the claim, which was the maximum allowed by his policy. A number of witnesses were called on Wakley's behalf, but he himself was prohibited by the then existing law from giving evidence.

The defence submitted that the claim was a fraud and that goods to the value specified had not been lost. In support of these allegations, the head foreman of the Hope Fire Assurance company and one of the appraisers, ignoring the evidence of theft, testified that they were unable to find certain imperishable goods said by the plaintiff to have been in the house at the time of the fire. Dr. Luke, who had attended Wakley after his escape from the burning house, deposed that the wounds could not have bled much and would not have accounted for all the discoloration of his shirt. Thus "refuting" Samuel Parker's "gushing" blood. In support of Luke, a Bow Street Runner produced a dummy wearing Wakley's blood-stained clothes to show that the cuts in the shirt, coat and waistcoat did not coincide with the cuts in the skin. However, his evidence collapsed under cross-examination.

The jury showed no hesitation in finding in Wakley's favour and he recovered the full amount of his cover of £1,200 with costs of £281.10.0d. The balance of his expenses was defrayed by public subscription. It is noteworthy that at least one of the jurors made a contribution as well as the son of the auditor of the Hope Fire Assurance Company.

Despite the vindication Wakley had to face the fact that his practice had entirely disappeared during the 10 months of his enforced recuperation. It took a further two months before he could even begin to commence in practice again, this time in the more down-market Norfolk Street off the Strand. He was now a controversial figure and although the allegation against him of arson was outrageous, it was several times revived by unscrupulous opponents. Indeed, on June 21, 1826 he obtained £100 damages from Dr. James Johnson, a former naval physician, for a libel in his journal the *Medico-Chirurgical Review* which compared Wakley with Lucifer, called him a firebrand and spoke of "extinguishing debts by means of fire-engines".

In the meantime Wakley's wife expressed a strong dislike of the neighbourhood of Norfolk Street and of the class of patients he had acquired there. She went so far as to beg him to leave and if necessary to discontinue his practice as a surgeon. He declined to leave but he did agree to relinquish his practice. Whether this was in response to his wife's entreaties or because other influences were beginning to enter his life is not clear. It was probably something of both.

The latter was a likely factor since it was about this time that Wakley had come under the radical influence of William Cobbett, who also thought the Cato Street conspirators had designs on his life. William Cobbett is, of course, a celebrated figure in English history, referred to by Carlyle as the prototype John Bull. He was born in 1763, the son of a small farmer of Farnham in Surrey who kept an inn, "The Jolly Farmer". In his early years he became in turn a gardener, an attorney's clerk and an army serjeant-major. After leaving the army he attempted to expose the military peculation he had come across and as a result was forced to flee to France. He later lived in America where he taught English to French emigrants, including Talleyrand, and became involved in Tory politics. It was at this time that he made repeated attacks on the radical Joseph Priestley and wrote a scornful biography of Tom Paine. He also started a number of highly popular, if short-lived, journals under the pseudonym of "Peter Porcupine".

Like Wakley, Cobbett drew upon himself a number of libel actions. One of these was for alleging that Dr. Benjamin Rush, a prominent physician and political figure, had bled George Washington to death. To avoid the consequences he returned to England armed with a hatred of democracy and a pungent patriotism. He soon launched his famous weekly paper, the *Political Register,* and founded the *Parliamentary Debates.* The Register was started as an extreme patriotic paper but Cobbett, like Winston Churchill later, was willing to change his allegiance and as his views modified it served different purposes at different times. During its 30-year life it was based solely on Cobbett's own personality and thinking. Ultimately it was to have a great deal to do with winning the industrial workers for the cause of radical parliamentary reform. At times it sold 60,000 copies a week. It was dubbed "Twopenny Trash" by Cobbett's enemies but this was a title he himself soon embraced with open arms.

For his denunciation of the flogging of English soldiers for demanding arrears of pay, Cobbett was imprisoned for two years and fined £2,000. These penalties ruined him. The fine was heavy and it did not help that he spent freely to purchase a degree of good living in prison. As a result he was left with no alternative but to sell his farm in Hampshire and dispose of the *Parliamentary Debates* to Hansard, whose name they still bear.

He managed to keep the *Register* going from prison, however, and in the ensuing period of political repression became the most influential spokesman of the working class, for whom he spoke in Parliament when he was elected for Oldham after the passing of the Reform Bill in 1832.

He was a brilliant writer who dedicated his later years to social betterment, and many of his works, including *Rural Rides,* have become English classics. His friendship with Wakley lasted until his death in 1835. His influence is clearly marked in Wakley's early writings and activities on behalf of the working class and later in his work in Parliament for a wider constituency.

However, the extent of Cobbett's influence on the founding of Wakley's *Lancet* is conjectural. He certainly played a significant role in the early issues of the journal. And Sprigge and Charles Brook both thought the inspiration was Cobbett's. But Dr. Mary Bostetter of Seattle, who possesses many of Wakley's own papers, has revealed the most potent influence in her essay, *The Journalism of Thomas Wakley.* There she shows that it was Dr. Walter Channing of Boston, a co-founder of the *New England Journal of Medicine and Surgery* in 1811, who encouraged, advised and gave financial help to Wakley in founding *The Lancet.*

CHAPTER 3

MEDICAL MAYHEM

The Lancet

In his own profession Wakley was already concerned that men could practise medicine without any qualification whatever and he became appalled by the open nepotism and jobbery he saw practised by many of the leading surgeons. At one point, in May 1824, Sir Astley Cooper, speaking of the surgeons of the Borough Hospitals had exclaimed: "Are they men I could possibly feel disposed to injure? Mr. Travers was my apprentice, Mr. Green is my godson, Mr. Tyrrell is my nephew, Mr. Key is my nephew, Mr. Morgan was my apprentice." And he forgot to mention Bransby Cooper, also his nephew. In an attempt to secure the remedy of this and many other abuses and at the same time to advance medical science, Wakley founded *The Lancet,* primarily as a campaigning journal, on Sunday October 5, 1823. In this enterprise he was wise enough to enlist the enthusiastic support of Cobbett, William Lawrence F.R.S. and James Wardrop.

Lawrence, afterwards Sir William Lawrence, Bart. (1783-1867) was a dazzling scholar and splendid lecturer who, unusually for that time, made a complete study of the principles and practice of surgery. A Fellowship of the Royal Society and important hospital appointments came to him in quick succession, including Professor of Anatomy at the Royal College of Surgeons. However, some of his attacks on received theories so infuriated John Abernethy, to whom he had been apprenticed, that the latter endeavoured to publicly humble him by describing him as "one of a party of modern sceptics, co-operating, in the diffusion of their noxious notions, with a no less terrible brand of French physiologists for the purpose of demoralizing mankind."

In reply Lawrence claimed a complete right of freedom of thought for men of science. He also went out of his way to identify himself publicly with the radical political movement by subscribing £10 to the fund for the defence of William Hone, who was tried (and acquitted) for writing a political parody on the Book of Common Prayer. Lawrence's enemies were active, however, and certain of his lectures were declared blasphemous by the Lord Chancellor, Lord Eldon. In consequence he was suspended from his Bridewell and Bethlem hospitals appointments. It was at this point in his career that he became a valued contributor to the new *Lancet*, although he was to desert Wakley later to join the Council of the Royal College.

James Wardrop (1782-1869) was a sufficiently brilliant surgeon for the Prince Regent to appoint him his surgeon-extraordinary. But this action only enraged the leaders of the profession in London. They saw Wardrop as an Edinburgh interloper and, abusing their monopoly, had every London hospital close its doors to him. In response he opened his own hospital in West London and continued to receive further royal favours.

It should also be mentioned that Wakley was less wise to accept the assistance of James Greenacre (1785-1837) who was eventually hanged as the "Camberwell murderer" and Daniel Whittle Harvey (1786-1863) who was in turn an allegedly fraudulent solicitor, a debarred barrister, a radical M.P. and for 23 years a distinguished Commissioner for the Metropolitan Police. In 1822 he founded *The Sunday Times* which he sold at a profit in 1833, but was generally regarded as being an unsavoury character.

These first three then were the men who gave the main support to Wakley and his new journal. Cobbett gave guidance in the framing of policy, Lawrence supplied first-class scientific articles and Wardrop had a ready pen to supply wit and venom in lampoons at the expense of the leaders of the profession. Of course their own motives and interests were also involved but they undoubtedly helped Wakley in his primary objects which were to publicize advances in medical knowledge which the hospitals were in the habit of keeping to themselves and to expose the corruption prevalent in the hospitals and other medical bodies. Before *The Lancet* was founded not a single clinical lecture was delivered in any of the hospitals in London, and no reports of cases which occurred in them were published. The name *Lancet* was chosen deliberately because, he wrote, "a lancet can be an arched window to let in the light or it can be a sharp surgical instrument to cut out the dross and I intend to use it in both senses." With these aims kept within his sights at all times Wakley set out to ensure that he was master of the new project. With the loss of his practice and the encouragement of his wife, he had sufficient time to devote to the task; that he also had the necessary talent quickly became evident.

In his first preface, Wakley outlined the policy of the new journal. He wrote:

We hope the age of *Mental Delusion* has passed and that mystery and concealment will no longer be encouraged. Indeed we trust that mystery and ignorance will shortly be considered synonymous. Ceremonies, and signs, have now lost their charms; hieroglyphics, and serpents, their power to deceive ... man studies with the greater attention and assiduity the constitutions of his horses and dogs and learns all their peculiarities; whilst of the nature of his own species he is totally uninformed ... acquirements in medical learning would furnish him with a test whereby he could detect and expose the impositions of ignorant practitioners.

There was plenty of variety in the first 36-page issue of *The Lancet,* which was published at sixpence. A lecture given by Sir Astley Cooper, but not contributed by him, occupied eight pages in the place of honour. There were reports of cases of clinical interest and of operations that had fatal terminations. There were dramatic criticisms and a political article, probably inspired or written by Cobbett, in which the younger Pitt was ridiculed and accused of having been "the political coxcomb, running after wild impracticable schemes, regardless of everything but the gratification of his own senseless, remorseless and petty ambitions." Robert Southey, the Poet Laureate, was referred to as "a sack-hunting hypocritical rhymer". Another excellent feature, undoubtedly inspired by Lawrence, and early incorporated in *The Lancet,* was a special section entitled "Foreign Department", in which new methods of treatment and accounts of operations were reported. This represented a serious attempt to keep the readers acquainted with what was going on in other countries.

With *The Lancet* Wakley now proceeded to raise controversy into an art. In the end, however, his achievement with it was to produce a settled policy of medical reform.[1] Editorials were written in Wakley's controversial and campaigning style. New discoveries in medicine were reported. Frequent articles appeared on the causes and treatment of many diseases of the mind and body. Campaigns were initiated to improve the standards and qualifications of apothecaries and surgeons as well as conditions in hospitals. Quacks and myths were exposed and destroyed. Over many years at least three important clinical lectures were published in each issue. After all, medical men and students were hardly likely to purchase a purely campaigning paper.

The journal's light relief was also close to Wakley's heart. Theatrical criticisms arose from his deep love of the stage which may also account for much of his histrionic style,

1. Even more than a century later in 1946 when a battle royal raged between the British Medical Association and Minister of Health, Aneurin Bevan, over the introduction of the National Health Service, only *The Lancet,* of all the medical journals, was able to take an objective view of what was involved.

although it was of course more common then than today. He was also an enthusiastic chess player and would exercise his mind with problems on a board at his side whilst editing his journal. Thus *The Lancet* became the first paper of any kind to publish chess problems and accounts of games. Nonetheless, after two years of publication, these items were reluctantly dropped. The reason was that the paper, with a regular readership of more than 4,000, had grown considerably in authority and had a demanding battle on its hands with the hospital authorities. However, he continued the good-humoured Friday night editorial meetings where, with a few loyal and enthusiastic supporters, including Cobbett, he would circulate the punch and plan the next number.

Sir Astley Cooper was to be attacked by Wakley not only for his nepotism but also for his ignorance of up-to-date surgical know-how. If, he wrote, Sir Astley stood self-convicted on his oath in a court of justice of such ignorance, what security had the public for the knowledge of the juniors of his family. Such a system of nepotism, he said, was foul and stunk to heaven. "Human life is sacrificed to it; medical science is sacrificed to it; the character and responsibility of the profession are sacrificed to it." To add insult to injury, Sir Astley also "treated" by post patients he could not possibly examine, although it must be said he was not alone in this.

However, not all was fire and brimstone in the relations between the antagonists. As we have seen, in the first issue of *The Lancet* Wakley had published a lecture of Sir Astley's without his permission but over his name. This was followed by others. As the first few issues of the journal gave no indication of the identity of its editor Sir Astley was completely in the dark as to who was responsible. He must have made an inspired guess, however, for he called on Wakley in the guise of a patient and, in a lucky moment, found his former pupil in the act of correcting the proofs of such a lecture. So pleased was he with the success of his ruse that his rage subsided into laughter and he agreed to Wakley continuing to publish his lectures in return for an undertaking that his name would be omitted. After all, as he justifiably complained to his students: "Though I did not [object to] the publication of my lectures I felt myself disgraced and degraded by my name forever appearing in the diurnal press ... this looked so much like quackery, so much like puffing, that I am unable to describe to you how much it annoyed me." He also asked Wakley to discontinue publishing details of hospital operations, but Wakley thought them too important to agree.

Attacking the Medical Oligarchy

An early offensive against the medical establishment had come in a series of biting articles on what Wakley called "hole-and-corner surgery". In them he described three surgeons who had ordered his exclusion from St. Thomas's Hospital as "The Three Ninny-hammers" - a nickname earlier dignified by Sterne and Swift. It needs to be emphasized, however, that these were more than personal attacks. Behind them lay Wakley's determination to force improvements in the standards of the surgeons as well as injecting a degree of democracy into their institutions. Then, on October 9, 1824, he accused one of them, Frederick Tyrrell, of literary piracy and professional incompetence. Apparently Tyrrell copied Sir Astley Cooper's lectures from *The Lancet* and published them as the only true version. But Wakley also exposed a post-mortem examination of a patient on whom Tyrrell claimed to have operated successfully. Heading his article "The Real Simon Pure" Wakley openly invited the action for libel which duly followed and was heard by Lord Chief Justice Best on February 25, 1825.

Wakley's counsel was Henry Brougham, later to become a

law-reforming Lord Chancellor. Brougham was already a celebrated Whig who had first made a name for himself as counsel by his defence of John Hunt and John Leigh Hunt in two prosecutions for seditious libel in their newspaper, *The Examiner.* The first trial, on January 22, 1811, arose from an article opposing flogging in the army, an issue on which Wakley was later to have a decisive influence. Brougham secured an acquittal and even the Judge, Lord Ellenborough, admitted his speech was remarkable for "great ability, eloquence and manliness". However, in the second trial, in 1812, when he unsuccessfully defended the Hunts against the Prince Regent, Lord Ellenborough, perhaps more concerned with the title of the plaintiff, avowed that Brougham was "inoculated with all the poison of the libels".

Brougham was a fearless and energetic advocate, although not entirely effective with a jury. His many qualities excited great admiration early in his career both in the country and in the House of Commons. And his fame knew no bounds after his renowned speeches in defence of Queen Caroline in 1820 and on law reform in 1828 and, not least, his creative role in the enactment of the Reform Act, 1832. Indeed, many thought he might become prime minister until, when the powerful member for Yorkshire, he was persuaded by distrustful colleagues to quit the House of Commons for the Chancellorship. His mother had, in fact, pleaded with him: "Do not be tempted to leave the House of Commons ... throw not away the great position you have raised yourself to - a position greater than any that could be bestowed by King or Minister." Nevertheless the King and Ministers were determined to curtail the power of one who had earned the nickname "Wicked Shifts" for his disloyalty and untruthfulness. In the event he put party loyalty first and although not destined to enjoy possession of the Great Seal for long, his tenure as Lord Chancellor was marked by a series of inspired legal reforms. Something of the forensic style of the times may be gleaned by an extract from the action of *Tyrrell* v. *Wakley*. Comparing Tyrrell's reports with those in *The Lancet* Brougham's comments brought on continuous laughter in court.

Here again is the incorrect account of *The Lancet,* he said, "certainly the formation of matter will be attended with a slight fever, but not of the hectic kind; the tongue will be clean, the pulse very little affected, and the person very slightly deranged; but after an opening is made into the part constitutional irritation sometimes comes on and life is then endangered." A most inaccurate representation of that worthy, learned, and skilful man, Sir Astley Cooper, which he (Sir Astley Cooper) could not bear to read - which haunted him every time he heard the name of *The Lancet* - he was punctured every time he heard it. "So", says he, "I will send to Mr. Tyrrell, he is an accurate man, he will not publish such trash; I will send for good Mr. Tyrrell, my 'Squire in medical knight-errantry', and he will publish what I say," so he sends for Mr. Tyrrell, and he says, "Mr. Tyrrell, there is sixpence for you, Mr. Tyrrell; go and lay it out in a way that is most calculated to correct the errors of *The Lancet."* And then with this sixpence he (Mr. Tyrrell) goes and purchases a number of *The Lancet* and tries the remedy of giving a correct account of what Sir Astley Cooper said; and, in order to do that, he gives you the full correct account: "Certainly the formation of matter will be attended by a slight fever, but not of the hectic kind; the tongue will be clean, the pulse very little affected, and the person very slightly deranged; but after an opening is made into the part constitutional irritation sometimes comes on and life is then endangered." As much alike as ever two peas were! Indeed, no two peas were so much alike.

Brougham dealt in a similarly ironic style with the case of Thomas Denman, who had died after an operation which Tyrrell had performed:

> A man is sent to hospital, Brougham said, with a compound fracture of the skull ... a battle begins, and then comes the skilful and powerful hand of our great champion, Mr. Tyrrell; and he, by the skill of his movements, by his extraordinary perseverances and able tactics, soon brought the thing to a successfull issue. He thought he had watched his enemy like a good and skilful commander, and fairly beaten him out of the field. So he thought and said on September 20; but unfortunately death in the end out-generalled him, and obtained the victory two days after the hasty proclamation of the good doctor's triumph. The fact was that while the plaintiff was gazetting his own promotion, while he was indulging in the fond aspirations of his own conquest, while he was making bonfires and letting off gunpowder - in the midst of rejoicing in came Death upon his patient, by a sort of lateral movement, opened his trenches, and, notwithstanding the formidable array of hospital weapons, bore away the palm of victory; horse, foot and dragoons; and left the poor doctors in dismay and discomfiture.

Although Brougham's style was better suited to his own time than it would be today he could not win over the jury who found for Tyrrell and awarded damages of £50. Wakley accused the Judge of prejudice and of disgraceful remarks in his address to the jury but the record does not support him.

The surgeon-teachers charged their students as much as £5 a time to attend their lectures and proved to be less amenable than Sir Astley Cooper when they saw their lectures published in *The Lancet* for sixpence. After all they collected substantial totals in tuition fees, virtually in perpetuity. Students were obliged to attend the lectures of five designated surgeons to obtain the certificates which alone gave entry to examinations and the teachers were also the examiners. Hence it was possible to purchase certificates and pass the examination without being adequately qualified to practise on an unsuspecting public. Not surprisingly, on behalf of these surgeons, and with their backing, John Abernethy, senior surgeon at St. Bartholomew's Hospital, took up the cudgels. As a first step he ordered the gas lamps in the lecture theatre at Bart's to be extinguished to foil the anonymous *Lancet* reporter. Despite the gloom the lecture was published since he overlooked the fact that William Lawrence, his assistant surgeon, had access to his notes. In any event he had not changed the content of his lectures in 37 years!

As a consequence, on December 10, 1824, Abernethy moved in the Court of Chancery for an injunction to restrain Wakley from publishing his lectures. The Lord Chancellor, Lord Eldon, came close to giving judgment against *The Lancet* without hearing the case on the ground that the lectures were delivered in a personal capacity to private pupils. Then, when counsel for the publishers submitted that it was the surgeon's public duty to deliver surgical teaching in a public place for the public good he relented and refused to grant an injunction. Wakley published 28 of Abernethy's lectures and he pushed the latter to further action in May 1825 when he wrote: "Mr. Abernethy may possibly have vanity enough to suppose that we shall reprint his lectures ... on this point his mind may be perfectly at ease; our pages have already been obscured with his hypothetical nonsense during six tedious months, and when we read the proof of his last paragraph we felt relieved of a most intolerable incubus." In the following month Abernethy made a second application when the Chancellor, true to his reputation, changed his mind again and granted the injunction, holding that the lectures could not be published for profit. That set a precedent which held until the Copyright Act of 1911.

Nevertheless, Wakley once more had the last word when his injunction was dissolved after he had insisted that it was monstrous for Abernethy to claim to have both the exclusive right to lecture as a public official (he was a member of the Court of Examiners of the Royal College of Surgeons) and the protection due to a private lecturer.

One of Wakley's campaigns which involved a series of specific attacks on malpractices in the hospitals culminated, on March 29, 1828, in a public description of a fatally bungled operation of lithotomy (cutting of a stone in the bladder) by Bransby Blake Cooper. Cooper was a surgeon at Guy's and a nephew of Sir Astley Paston Cooper. Wakley frankly asserted that Bransby Cooper was "surgeon because he was nephew". With great detail, he painted a terrifying picture of incompetency, want of skill, lack of nerve, and want of heart. Details given of Bransby Cooper's fumbling and groping were grotesque. In fact, claimed Wakley, the patient, who was to have been operated on by Sir Astley, had been cut up and murdered in an operation that took an hour instead of a few minutes.

As was normal with this type of operation the patient was bound to the operating table with his hands tied to his feet and his knees to his neck. Bransby Cooper was heard complaining that he could not reach the bladder with his finger and asking bystanders if anyone had a long finger! After receiving another instrument he exclaimed: "Now I have it. Good God! I can hear the stone but the forceps won't touch it - oh dear! oh dear!" When the patient, who was not under general anaesthetic, cried out, "Oh, let it go - pray let it keep in!" Bransby Cooper startingly replied: "You were brought here to have the stone removed and removed it shall be if you die upon the table." Although a strong country labourer the patient died indeed the following day and the post-mortem revealed internal injuries caused during the operation.

Bransby Cooper sued Wakley for libel. The case was heard in the King's Bench at Westminster Hall in 1829, before the ageing but benevolent Lord Tenterden (formerly Abbott, L.C.J.) sitting with a special jury, and excited widespread interest. Indeed, some officers of the Court obtained fees of a sovereign a time for procuring seats for spectators. And such was the struggle to gain admittance that some barristers lost their wigs and coats were torn. After the trial William Cobbett was to pillory the Judge in his *Policital Register* for allowing to sit on the Bench with him a number of surgeons, including Sir Astley Cooper, who were to descend into the witness box to give evidence against Wakley. "Let us hope", he concluded roundly, "that before we get a reform of the 'collective' this practice of perching prosecutors, or the witnesses of prosecutors, upon the Bench will be discontinued."

Wakley wished to address the jury himself. This meant that his counsel, Henry Brougham and Fitzroy Kelly, could take no part in the trial, but they continued to advise him. Wakley commenced by claiming both the right to open the case and have the general reply on the ground that it was on him that lay the burden of proving Cooper's lack of skill. Since this had never occurred before in cases of libel and Tenterden's decision might prove to be an important precedent he consulted two other Judges who were sitting in an adjoining court and Wakley won his point. It was to prove an important right for defendants and Wakley claimed in *The Lancet:* "We maintained our point of law not only against Sir James Scarlett (prosecuting counsel) but against the opinion of our own counsel and we gained it." At the time Scarlett was Attorney-General in Wellington's Ministry and noted for his hounding of the radical press.

Wakley thereupon made his opening address and called his witnesses first. In his speech to the jury Wakley claimed the best of motives in publishing the report. His one desire, he said, was that the management of the hospitals should be efficient, and that only those possessing the highest professional skill should be elected to hold the senior medical and surgical staff appointments. His first witness was a surgeon, named Partridge, who had been present throughout the operation and considered *The Lancet* report to be accurate. Another surgeon agreed that the operation was completely mishandled. Wakley had also subpoenaed Sir Astley Cooper and he examined him both on the operation and on his stated view that to become a great surgeon a man must wade up to his neck in blood. Predictably Sir Astley accounted his nephew a good surgeon, although not yet excellent. In his turn Bransby Cooper called only one witness present at the operation to give evidence of his skill, despite the fact that 200 people had been there. Sir James Scarlett, smarting from his earlier defeat at the hands of a layman, denounced one of Wakley's witnesses as a hireling only to have Wakley retort that Sir James should remember that he was himself a hireling working for the sake of lucre. This proved to be merely an opening shot in Wakley's future attacks on the legal profession which was becoming quite unscrupulous in its efforts to gain control of the courtroom - a process which was to lead to the Judge and jury becoming umpires instead of participants in the trial as traditionally they had been.

True to his beliefs Wakley in his emotional final speech to the jury did not confine himself to the legal issues but called upon the jury to show by their verdict that the poor were not properly treated by such surgeons as Mr. Bransby Cooper. Give a verdict, he said, to satisfy the poor that they are not to be killed by surgeons at liberty to "wade and ride through blood up to their necks to eminence in the profession, like great generals."[2] When Wakley concluded and resumed his seat he won loud applause from various parts of the court, which was mirrored outside and in the press.

1. Even more than a century later in 1946 when a battle royal raged between the British Medical Association and Minister of Health, Aneurin Bevan, over the introduction of the National Health Service, only *The Lancet,* of all the medical journals, was able to take an objective view of what was involved.
2. Eyewitness account by J.F. Clarke in his *Autobiographical Recollections,* 55, 57.

Cooper obtained a verdict, but with only nominal damages of £100 instead of the £2,000 he had claimed. This virtually established Wakley's main contention of malpractice. In consequence his expenses were again met by public subscription. After the case Bransby Cooper published a report of the trial, from the notes of W.B. Gurney, a parliamentary shorthand writer, in which he alleged a conspiracy by Wakley and others against himself. Wakley, however, denied the allegation and had the last word in his own more detailed account of the trial, complete with diagrams of the instruments used in the operation. The facts spoke for themselves. It is an interesting sidelight on the characters of both men that they later became good friends.

The fame of *The Lancet* prospered on this and other vituperative disputes and its weekly circulation doubled to 8,000. Partly it was the open enmity and stormy exchanges which attracted interest. Sir Astley Cooper called *The Lancet,* the "Reptile Press". Sir Anthony Carlisle, senior surgeon at Westminster Hospital, whom Wakley had nicknamed "The Oyster" spoke to his students of the "notorious publication" which was a disgrace to the medical profession. Wakley also received unscrupulous personal abuse from the contemporary medical press who saw their own circulation and prestige threatened. The *Medical and Physical Journal,* for example, attacked Wakley's hospital reports as a monstrous breach of professional etiquette. Wakley retorted by describing its proprietor, Dr. Roderick Macleod as "Roderick the Goth" and the "Editor of the Gothic Absurdity".

Dr. Johnson and his *Medico-Chirurgical Review* we have already had occasion to notice. Then there was the *Medical Gazette* founded in 1827 solely to counter the influence of *The Lancet.* Founded by a number of hospital surgeons, Dr. Roderick Macleod left his Review to become *The Gazette's* editor and made no bones in print about his hatred of the policy of *The Lancet,* declaring that "a few years ago a set of literary plunderers broke in on the peace and quiet of our profession ... for profit." Wakley, aware that the aim of *The Gazette* was to ruin *The Lancet,* was stung to reply, "some despicable imitations of us have arisen, and *stunk,* and become extinguished .. one or two are still *emitting a little foetor."*

But all this name-throwing merely reflected the importance of the issues involved. Wakley had to inflict mayhem on his spurious opponents if his campaigns for root-and-branch reforms were not to fail ignominiously. And he was generally fair-minded, commended his "enemies" on occasion and, above all, was dedicated to improving the profession, expanding medical knowledge and securing adequate education for students. As a consequence he received considerable and widespread support.

Thus encouraged he accepted the responsibility and the challenge of a struggle to improve the Royal College of Surgeons of London - its full and restrictive title. In addition to the abuses already mentioned he turned his pen against the extraction by surgeons of £3,600 a year from poor students in lecture fees and the creation of a self-perpetuating monopoly of leadership in the Councillors of the College. So undemocratic was the College that the Master and small Court of Assistants were appointed for life and could appoint their own successors for life. Members were debarred from all decision-making absolutely. In fact they were treated with such contempt that they were not allowed to enter the College by the front doors and were reduced to using a miserable back entrance in Portugal Street. Consequently, early in 1826 Wakley convened a meeting of Members of the College to support a petition to the Crown. This was to call for either a new Charter or a Royal Commission to inquire into the working of the existing Charter. Over 1,200 attended what was the first public meeting of the Members ever to be held. Meeting at the Freemason's Tavern in London they found a prominent supporter in Joseph Hume MP, leader of the Radicals in the House of Commons. Hume had qualified as a surgeon in Edinburgh but entered politics after amassing a fortune of £40,000 whilst in the service of the East India Company, which he first joined as a ship's doctor.

By a large majority the meeting approved a Motion put by Wakley but his demands were not met at that stage. It was not until February 12, 1831, five years later, that any action followed. Wakley was then holding another meeting of members, this time in the theatre of the College, when he was requested by the authorities to leave. On his refusal to do so a number of Bow Street Runners were sent in to drag him out. Wakley was hit by a truncheon and, with his clothes torn about him, went to Bow Street court followed by a large and uproarious crowd. Here he charged his assailant before the chief magistrate, Sir Richard Birnie who, admitting his bias, refused Wakley a warrant.

Ever confident, Wakley then proposed to set up a London College of Medicine on democratic lines and with impartial examiners, which would produce all-round doctors and replace the Royal College of Surgeons, the Royal College of Physicians and the Worshipful Company of Apothecaries altogether. It was to be a "temple of light". However, his supporters wanted reform not a fresh start and the project failed to get off the ground. Even then it took another 12 years before Queen Victoria granted a new Charter for the Royal College of Surgeons of England as it was now to be styled. A new class of members, known as Fellows, was called into being from whom, and by whom, an enlarged Council was to be elected.

Blunders of Bats

During the first 10 years of its existence Wakley had constantly provoked a succession of angry collisions between *The Lancet* and members of the privileged groups in medicine. As a result he was frequently involved in proceedings for injunction in the Court of Chancery and libel actions in the King's Bench. He was also banned from entering St. Thomas's Hospital in May 1824 for describing Sir Astley Cooper's surgical team as "a party united to each other, not only by the amiable ties of consanguinity, but by the no less delightful vinculum of a common participation in £3,600 which they annually extract from the students." However this order was successfully evaded and most of his disputes he won. And there lies the point. At no time was Wakley interested in needless attacks on the hospitals or their officials. What he wanted was to bring them under democratic control, destroy nepotism and release the hospitals and the surgeons from restraints on research and free public discussion that would advance the whole profession of medicine. And to that end he described the leading surgeons as "Bats and Corruptionists" and in issue after issue of *The Lancet* he mercilessly revealed details of their failures in surgery and neglect of their hospital duties. One example is from a leading article in January 1829 under the heading "Blunders of Bats". He wrote:

The fruits of the corrupt system that prevails at our public hospitals, are seen in the numerous cases of ignorance and incompetency on the part of hospital functionaries, which have been recorded in public journals, though these, it must be admitted, are few indeed, compared with those which have actually occurred. These things shall no longer be concealed. We have seen a hale, athletic man, who supposed that he had a stone in his bladder, enter an operating theatre, where he was sounded with such violence that he was incapable of returning to his home. He was put to bed, violent inflammation came on, and he became delirious.

His bladder, as it was afterwards discovered, had been "pierced" by the sound; the scrotum and integuments at the lower part of the abdomen, "mortified"; in 10 days after the sounding his sufferings were terminated, and the unfortunate man, who entered the hospital sound, and hale and healthy, to seek advice for a complaint which existed only in his imagination, was dead, and perhaps dissected, before his family knew what had become of him. Such are the exploits of the men, who style themselves the heads of the profession. Another hospital surgeon mistook a pebble for a part of a man's knee-pan, though the man's knee-pan was entire, and nearly two inches from the pebble. Yet the same Hospital Bats, who swore the other day that an operation which they had not witnessed was scientifically performed - the same Hospital Bats, who are always on the alert to wing their way to a court of justice, when a colleague's skill is questioned - the same Bats, who like Day & Martin in the advertisements, are "ever anxious to prevent exposure" - swore also in the pebble case, that the patient had been scientifically treated.

Subsequently, in an editorial in the anniversary issue of October 1, 1931, Wakley reviewed the previous eight years of publication and stressed that *The Lancet* would triumph if it continued to devote itself to one object - the public good. "Principle is our motto", he declared, "and we are determined to succeed or perish." Utterly fearless of the consequences he then launched into a breathtaking attack entitled: "A Rare Whack at the Voracious Bats."

They aimed, he wrote, to put down *The Lancet* by threats, clamours, injunctions, indictments and all other contrivances of those haters of light, the "corrupt, avaricious, plundering, rapacious, dirty-minded BATS" (i.e., the leading surgeons). These Bats, he continued in stinging style, lived in idleness and luxury and were traders in "diploma-cy". They cruelly plundered medical students whom they did not educate but robbed in fees for medical certificates. Warming to his theme - if that were necessary - he asserted they performed in "Theatres of Sacrifice", were possessed of claws instead of hands and made sad use of the knife, often tearing off with force the diseased limbs of suffering patients which required in their removal much care and the greatest gentleness.

Fellows of the Royal College of Physicians did not escape his venom when he continued that the Archbishop of Canterbury was empowered to manufacture them by divine right. As for the Royal College of Surgeons, with 6,000 members and a self-perpetuating Council of 21 it was led by an oligarchy which had made it merely a warehouse for surgical diplomas. And, although Wakley did not mention them, it must be remembered that the Universities of Oxford and Cambridge set no better example. In those hallowed places the combined use of bribery and medieval regulations allowed students who had never studied medicine or even seen a patient or a hospital to qualify as Doctors of Medicine. Indeed, the Professor of Medicine at Cambridge was required to give a course of lectures each year but no incumbent of the post had lectured at all since the year 1700.

Wakley was also a frequent critic of the Society of Apothecaries which he dubbed "Rhurbarb Hall" and its governors "The Old Hags". His lively pen wrote of them: "The truth is, that these fellows are as ignorant as their own posters, and are only calculated to wield the pestles in the shop which they have opened in Bridge Street. A contemptible gang of Retail Druggists to legislate for the members of the Royal College of Surgeons and medical students. This is the 'march of intellect indeed'." They were, he added, "unlearned dealers in roots and syrups."

Time and success, however, were to change the opposition

to *The Lancet* into support. Wakley himself, conscious of the ever-growing reputation of his brilliant creation, became less vitriolic and sarcastic in his approach to others. Obituaries he published paid tribute to his erstwhile enemies. But he never surrendered his right to criticize on just occasion. And those who had denounced it most fiercely came to write for *The Lancet* and to praise it for its independence and its contribution to medical science. Wakley had at last succeeded in one of the major tasks on which he had set his heart.[3] From being virtually the property and inheritance of a small irresponsible oligarchy as well as engines of tyranny to students, the London hospitals and schools were transformed into comparatively open and free institutions with a healthy and active scientific life. Wakley's achievement had been brought about by initiative, genius and impassioned courage using as his weapons persuasion, invective and satire.

He himself had said, in September 1835, that the object of medical reformers was nothing less than the conservation of the public health. To this great aim it was necessary to bring the whole power and force of the science of medicine into operation. In the end he played a large part in setting that science in motion by shaking up the medical profession and its institutions. And the reputation of *The Lancet* in the ensuing years, and still today, is an enduring testimony to his success.

3.   Not all that Wakley wanted has yet been achieved in medicine. Despite considerable improvements the education of students is still unsatisfactory. A closed society of consultants remains. There is still difficulty in suing doctors for negligence and, sadly, funds are still woefully inadequate.

CHAPTER 4

THE ROTUNDISTS

Whilst Wakley was engaged in the conflicts described in the previous chapter the country was experiencing the economic and political upheavals that were to explode in the Reform Bill agitation of 1831. The reform movement, at first supported by Pitt in the 1780s, had been crushed in consequence of the horror aroused in England by the reign of terror in the French Revolution. Its rebirth was now overdue. The growing effects of the Industrial Revolution had made the House of Commons even less representative than before and there had arisen a new working class clamouring for the vote. Moreover, the expanding middle class, although largely without representation, had a new sense of power which was voiced by its champion James Mill.

Mill seemed to think that the "middling classes", as he often liked to call them, had guided the majority of the people throughout history and were the highest product of civilization. In the *Westminster Review* of January 1824 he had written of the middle class:

> It contains beyond all comparison, the greater proportion of the intelligence, industry, and wealth of the state. In it are the heads that invent, and the hands that execute; the enterprise that projects, and the capital by which those projects are carried into operation ... The people of the class below are the instruments with which they work; and those of the class above, though they may be called their governors, and may really sometimes seem to rule them, are much more often, more truly, and more completely under their control. In this country at least, it is this class which gives to the nation its character.

Mill generalized the experience of the people who made up that class, contributed to their understanding of their place in society and pointed the way forward for them. They had to destroy aristocratic rule if they were to command their inheritance and he called for an open attempt to replace aristocratic with middle-class political leadership of society. This was exactly what large numbers of the middle class wanted to hear. Times had changed and, not surprisingly, the demand for reform burst upon the scene with a fresh energy and sense of urgency.

Nevertheless, the Tories remained adamantly hostile. But Brougham and Lord John Russell were able to press ahead when a Whig government was elected in 1830. However, the prospect of success looked slim unless the middle class and the working class could unite to bring substantial pressure to bear and force a measure of reform through a reluctant House of Lords. To this end a large number of political unions were formed in many parts of the country to demand reform and the resultant agitation was particularly successful in Birmingham where for a time 25 political union debating clubs were meeting weekly. The middle-class union there was ably led by Thomas Attwood, the Birmingham banker and currency reformer and working-class support was also won.

On the other hand, some radical working-class elements wanted no alliance with the middle class and saw the awakening struggle as a means to press for a more extreme solution. They formed the National Union of the Working Classes on April 2, 1831, led, among others, by William Lovett who gave it a strong Owenite bias. The NUWC had a number of local branches outside London which were in contact with radical members of the Political Unions and it was to counter their influence that in October Francis Place decided to found a National Political Union to unite all the local unions and keep the NUWC at bay.

On October 9 the rejection of the Reform Bill by the House of Lords had been received in London as a national calamity. The Liberal *Morning Chronicle* appeared with black edges and there were many disorderly meetings. Indeed, police had great difficulty in preventing a large body of NUWC supporters from marching on Westminster. Less than three weeks later on October 27, Bristol went up in flames in riots in which the gaols were forced open, the town hall fired and the Bishop's palace burnt to the ground. Order was restored after several days only when the cavalry were rushed in. The castle at Nottingham was also burned, Derby gaol was sacked and angry crowds appeared on the streets of London where the King's carriage was mishandled. This extreme expression of the revival of spiritual and political life taking place among the middle and working classes transformed the situation. New battle lines were drawn which meant a fight to the finish with either reform or revolution triumphant. Place was extremely fearful of violent revolution and thought Wakley was prepared to countenance it.

Certainly talk of revolution was widespread and Home Office files bear witness to many disturbances taking place up and down the country. Pamphlets, leaflets and posters tumbled off the presses in profusion. Examples of propaganda abound. One poster headed, "Reform! or Revolution!!" urged, "The House of Lords have presumed to *reject the Bill* ... Will you submit that 200 individuals shall make slaves of millions." After calling for the creation of new peers its main message was: "Pay no more Taxes - Pay no more Tithes." And all backed by argument at a time when posters put a case with words rather than a visual image. Another poster, under a heading, "BLACKLIST", set out the names of the Lords who had voted against the Bill with figures of their wealth described as "Pickings". The issue of the *Republican* journal for November 1831 dated merely "November - Year of the People 1", cried

"Down With the Lords" and after referring to them as indescribable animals called for the abolition of the House of Lords as a public nuisance. On the other side were posters giving details for arrangements for the enrolment of Special Constables and a pamphlet by Joseph Sparrow entitled: "Reform not Revolution."

What prompted Wakley to join the battle is not clear and his participation is not even mentioned by his official biographer. Yet it was a significant phase in his life and an alignment which was to cause much disquiet to Francis Place. Wakley's old friend William Cobbett was, of course, delighted to be in the fray, but their paths do not appear to have crossed although he may have encouraged Wakley in the stand he took with the NUWC. Nevertheless it was logical for Wakley to extend his struggle for reform of the medical profession to that for more democracy in national life.

Most reformers thought the Whigs' Bill a crucial step forward although it did not meet all their demands, in particular the ballot. Their view was expressed in Brougham's famous slogan on the hustings: "The Bill, the whole Bill and nothing but the Bill." Wakley, however, whilst always having the most worthy objectives in mind, and living a respectable personal life, could be intemperate in his tactics and arguments when occasion demanded. Here then, ready-made for him, was the NUWC whose members were soon dubbed the "Rotundists" by those who considered its full title, and its activities, distasteful.

The Rotunda, as its name implies, was a large round building to be found in Blackfriars Bridge Road south of the Thames. Built originally as a riding school it was now owned by Richard Carlile, the much imprisoned radical printer, who issued from it the *Prompter* at 3d weekly. His politics may be summed up by his avowal that if moral resistance was not effectual, physical resistance was to be recommended whenever there was a prospect of its success. Nevertheless, he supported the Bill as a stepping stone to universal suffrage. Lectures were held at the Rotunda most evenings and on one occasion when Cobbett spoke not only was the hall filled but 3,000 men assembled outside. This then came to house the meetings of the NUWC - a place called by Carlile "the real House of Commons".

The Home Office files for the period contain an Opinion by counsel headed "Re The Rotunda". Apparently, in 1831, Solicitors Meymott & Son asked Mr. I. Gurney, a barrister of Lincoln's Inn, to advise on behalf of a magistrate who desired to close down the Rotunda. They informed counsel that it was a hotbed of sedition and blasphemy with Henry Hunt, Cobbett and Carlile among the main culprits. Their frequent meetings, it was alleged, caused annoyance to neighbouring residents and interrupted the thoroughfare in consequence of large numbers of people forming overflow meetings outside. Particularly offensive was the "Rev." Robert Taylor who, in the costume of a clergyman, gave blasphemous discourses to hundreds. Box seats at 6d and the gallery at 3d were both crowded to capacity. The magistrate had engaged a shorthand writer and the beadle to attend such meetings and obtain evidence. Could the magistrate, the solicitors asked counsel, close down the Rotunda? Mr. Gurney advised that he could proceed and convict under statute, viz. 39 Geo. 3 s. 15, but he thought such action would be imprudent as likely to lead to retaliation. Of what kind he did not say, merely recommending that the question be referred to the Home Secretary. Which, no doubt, is why the Opinion now lies in the vaults of the Public Record Office.

Place wrote that in 1831 the NUWC had some 500 members who each paid 1/2d a week for their card. There were also about 1,000 who paid only occasionally at times of great excitement, but who reckoned themselves members. Some dozen branches had been formed in various districts of London but the Rotunda was the important centre. Weekly public meetings were held there by the Union which, said Place, in confirmation of other reports, "would probably contain a thousand persons, and I have seen hundreds outside the doors for whom there was no room within." Other meeting places included the "Argyle Arms" in Argyle Street, the Chapel in Finsbury Square, the "Blind Beggar" in Bethnal Green, the "Duke of York" at Hammersmith, the "Yorkshire Grey" in Hampstead, the "Compasses" in Bermondsey and the Lecture Room in Theobalds Road. A clear indication of the extent to which the NUWC's activities in the capital stretched.

According to Place the programme of the NUWC called for an end to the system of exploitation of wage slaves by masters and proclaimed that everything produced belonged to those whose labour produced it and should be shared amongst them. There should be no accumulation of capital permitted to enable employment of others as labourers. And they considered that anyone who differed from them was a "political economist" and a bitter foe of the working class. As a consequence, he said, the Rotundists were not interested in the General Election or in support for the middle class to secure reform. To Place this was an approach leading to violent revolution and a clear threat to the future of the middle class. He declared, with feeling, that the Rotundists were "perfectly atrocious, resolute, reckless rascals" who desired nothing less than insurrection. Yet, at least in Nottingham, his NPU itself was reported to be "rapidly arming".

In fact, the official declaration issued by the NUWC, and bearing some resemblance to both the US Constitution and the programme of Gerard Wynstanley's "Diggers" in the seventeenth century, proclaimed that all men were born equally free and demanded manhood suffrage. All men, it continued, had certain natural, inherent and inalienable rights on which all governments should be founded. All property, honestly acquired, was sacred but all laws should be for the common benefit, protection and security of all the people. Other demands, including the ballot, were similar to those made by the successors to the Rotundists in the People's Charter, which itself owed a great deal, as we shall see, to Thomas Wakley, MP.

Reform or Revolution

Notwithstanding the views of Place, in October 1831, after the rejection of the Bill by the House of Lords, a magnificent procession of 70,000 marched on Westminster. Here a deputation of the NUWC waited on Lord Melbourne, the Home Secretary, with an Address praying His Majesty not to create any new peers but to abolish the House of Lords and introduce universal suffrage with vote by ballot. Melbourne indicated that he could not present the Address to His Majesty because of its strong language. His Majesty, he said, might as well hang a man without trial as attempt to suppress the House of Lords. The deputation replied that the Lords had already been tried and were convicted as traitors to their King and country and ought to be abolished, which appears to have left Melbourne speechless. Meanwhile outside, all the nearby shops were shut and white scarves of the Rotundists were everywhere to be seen. The NUWC appeared to be about to assume the leadership of the working class in London.

Place called a meeting of the National Political Union at the famous Crown & Anchor tavern in the Strand for October 31. The purpose was to recruit members, which was in accord with the tradition of the time that new political organizations should be formed at public meetings. According to the *Morning Chronicle* some 2,000 people attended. The tavern was crowded to suffocation with a strong contingent of Rotundists present. Place complained of fluent, but remarkably ignorant, speeches filled with bitter notions of animosity against everybody who did not concur in their absurdities. Because of the overcrowding the chairman, Sir Francis Burdett, asked Wakley to call upon those inside and outside the building to adjourn to Lincoln's Inn Fields. Here the crowd swelled to 20,000.

A resolution was duly proposed that the NPU be formed and a Council elected with two objects. The first was to secure effective representation of the middle and working classes in the House of Commons. The second, to preserve peace and order to guard against any disorder which enemies of the people might endeavour to bring about. According to Lovett's autobiography Place and his supporters managed to drown out Lovett and Cleave but not Wakley. In the "debate" Wakley called for unity. The common object, he said, was to obtain for all men equal justice and equal rights. In contrast to Place's charge of his destructiveness, Wakley next issued an invitation to "a marriage of the middle and working classes".

But from his own standpoint Place knew the menace to his plans that Wakley represented. He had not long to wait. Pursuing the issue to its logical end, Wakley drove Place to despair by moving an amendment to the resolution to provide that 50% of those to be elected to the Council of the NPU be drawn from the working-class and 50% from the middle class. Place was aghast. He had visions of middle class support for the NPU dissolving into thin air. Although he wanted the classes to present a common front he firmly believed leadership must be, and must be seen to be, in the hands of the middle class and himself with the artisans in a purely supporting role, not as equal allies.

Mild and kind as ever, Lovett was swamped but eventually managed to make himself heard and proposed full manhood suffrage. Still no one involved could bridge the gap and accept women's suffrage although in another setting Macaulay had publicly criticised James Mill for just this deficiency. John Cleave, a former sailor but now a keeper of a coffee shop, supported Lovett passionately and added that there could be nothing but full reform or revolution. There was some hissing and they were accused, accurately of course, of being Rotunda men. Sir Francis Burdett, MP for Westminster and a long-standing champion of Reform, chose this moment to retire from the half-formed NPU in disgust at the turn things were taking. Shortly after the meeting Roebuck, the Radical MP for Bath, and other allies of Place urged him to agree to Wakley's amendment but he adamantly refused.

Place now set out to undo the damage he conceived Wakley's amendment had produced in the minds of the middle class, and to persuade them to join the NPU. Another meeting was called, this time for November 10, at which a Council would be elected. Wakley said he would stand for the Council provided 50% of its members were drawn from the working class. This, said Place, would increase animosities and he described Wakley as particularly obnoxious, but admitted it was impossible to proceed without him. He was less than pleased when Wakley was elected on to the committee formed to devise plans for the election of the Council.

In the meantime the NUWC called a meeting to be held outside White Conduit House in White Conduit Street at 1 p.m. on November 7. Handbills advertising the meeting were distributed in large numbers and placed in the windows of many small shopkeepers. They proclaimed the aims of the Union and indicated that Wakley would take the chair. Place commented bitterly that Wakley and the Rotunda men had called the meeting to see how far they could rely on the mob for mischief. He maintained that at a meeting in a coffee house in Fleet Street near Temple Bar, held to organize the White Conduit meeting, it was proposed that everyone who attended should bring a 20" stave as a weapon. There is little truth in the allegations although Wakley undoubtedly wished to test the Rotunda strength. But at all times he wanted the NUWC to be law-abiding and he opposed the use of staves. In any event the possession of arms - let alone staves - was even encouraged and spoken of approvingly by *The Times* which, on November 1, after giving a full report of the Lincoln's Inn Fields' meeting, editorially thundered; "We say to our fellow subjects, organize and arm." This was, of course, the time when the preoccupation with the Reform Bill of its editor, Thomas Barnes, earned the newspaper the title of "The Thunderer". However, the Rotundists saw a middle-class "National Guard" as a threat to themselves, and in consequence the *Poor Man's Guardian* proposed an alternative "Popular Guard" for England. Notwithstanding Wakley's peaceful stance in all this excitement, one citizen wrote to Lord Melbourne on November 7 accusing Wakley of treason and urging him to act against him before it was too late.

In the event the meeting was postponed when Melbourne circularized the magistrates and pronounced its objects illegal, seditious and perhaps treasonable. According to the *Poor Man's Guardian* the Committee were to be seized as traitors. It should be remembered that at the time treason was punishable with the medieval horror of being hanged, drawn and quartered whilst being kept alive. A contributory factor in securing the postponement was the fact that the government, scared by the riots in Bristol, marched a considerable number of troops into Islington and swore in hundreds of special constables. Although *The Times* blamed Sir Charles Wetherell, Bristol's Recorder for the riots, Wakley shrewdly assessed the dangers of proceeding precipitately after the arson there and in Nottingham. Acting with speed he published on the day of the meeting a huge poster over his name, from "Bedford Square, Sunday Morning", calling for prudence and postponement of the meeting on the ground that the "sanguinary Boroughmongers" intended to make the working class victims of a plot for the forcible overthrow of the government and the entire destruction of peace and social order. And for good measure he added, "Remember the KING himself is on your side and has declared unequivocally for REFORM." As indeed he had. Wakley was heeded and the meeting did not materialize, but as a postscript the *Morning Chronicle* reported that on the following day a substantial meeting at the Rotunda was attended by over 1,000 people, many armed with wooden truncheons and wearing tri-colour cockades.

Meanwhile Place, with his usual assiduity, was busy selecting members for the NPU from those who were attending the Crown and Anchor to enrol, and rejecting all who did not denounce the NUWC. Thus, by the time the Council came to be elected on November 10 Place, on his own admission, had carefully packed the meeting of some 1,500 people and Wakley, who was hissed when he spoke, failed to secure election. His petulant response was to declare that he could not spare the time to be on the Council, to which a section of the crowd responded with "We don't want you". This stung Wakley to exclaim gratuitously that he would never form part of any society to which Henry Hunt belonged - "that heartless and cold-blooded traitor"; so the venom was not all on one side. Nevertheless, to some extent Wakley was the victor since even Place with his vetted membership was unable to prevent the election of 52% of the Council from members of the working class. Although for the time being the NUWC was now isolated.

Subsequently, on December 12, Lord John Russell introduced a third Reform Bill and its Second Reading in the Commons was carried by a large majority on December 31. Then in the New Year the government, facing a new threat, called for a National Fast Day to be held on March 21 in response to a widespread epidemic of cholera. The declared purpose was to beseech God to remove the cholera. Undoubtedly the epidemic was causing widespread alarm. Home Office files are full of reports relating to it from all over the country and the *Lancet* carried numerous articles about the disease. The Rotundists, promptly ridiculed the government's "solution", which lay in its own hands not the Almighty's, calling it a National Farce Day. To establish their point, and exhibit their strength, they decided to call a demonstration for the same day. At 11 a.m. they assembled and some 100,000 people paraded the streets in a procession carrying at its head a loaf of bread and a round of beef with the inscription "The True Cure for the Cholera". This went on until 4 p.m. when the protesters were asked to go home to feast. Lovett, Watson and Benbow were arrested as leaders of the procession but were acquitted at their trial on May 16.

There can be no doubt that the Rotundists were correct and that the cholera was caused by poverty and the lack of even the most elementary sanitation in towns and cities. As the medical officers of the Holborn Union reported, if the cesspools of London were joined together they would have formed a channel 10 miles long, 50 feet wide and six feet deep. Together they supplied the Thames daily with 7,000 loads of poisonous filth. Hunger and disease were both rife in many districts of London and in his autobiography William Lovett describes pathetic scenes of want and deprivation when he accompanied Wakley on one of his investigations in Spitalfields. He describes the houses they visited as hotbeds of disease, with fever and hunger ravaging the dwellers within them. These were scenes Wakley was to recall throughout his life. It may cause no surprise to learn that the inhabitants of the district were cold in their reception of the visitors. However, Lovett points out that Wakley's fame as a medical reformer turned distrust into warm acceptance when he was seen and that Wakley lost no time in giving medical assistance where he could.

It was at this time also that John Martin, the celebrated Romantic artist, was expressing in his magnificently awesome paintings the awakening conscience of the middle class at the appalling conditions brought about by the Industrial Revolution. As part of his social criticism, which was by no means confined to his paintings, prints of which were sweeping the country in an intense fervour, he also produced far-reaching plans and designs for the improvement of sewage and sanitation in the Metropolis.

The Third Reading of the Reform Bill was carried the day after the National Fast Day. A sense of the feelings of some members of the working class about the Bill can be gauged from an article in an unstamped issue of the *Poor Man's Guardian* in November 1931 which said: The Bill "is the most illiberal, the most tyrannical, the most abominable, the most infamous, the most hellish measure that ever could or can be proposed ... I therefore conjure you to prepare your coffins, if you have the means. You will be starved to death by thousands if this Bill passes, and thrown on the dunghill or on to the ground naked like dogs." On the other side Edward Gibbon Wakefield published a scurrilous but popular pamphlet entitled: "householders in danger from the populace" in which Rotunda radicals and London thieves were classed together as special objects of dread to all householders. "These", he said, "will be the fighting men of our revolution, if we must have one." Not to be outdone, both the Whig and Tory presses denounced the Rotundists as revolutionists, pickpockets and incendiaries contemplating an attack on every possessor of property and uprooting all law and order. As we shall see Wakley, with his newspaper the *Ballot,* opposed both these extremes in his battle for the Bill.

Under the threat of the creation of new peers the House of Lords passed the Bill on April 13 but then attempted to scuttle it in Committee in May. The response was shattering and brought the NPU and the Rotundists into joint action for the first time. One issue alone of *The Times* (May 16) gave lengthy reports of meetings in Birmingham, Leeds, Manchester, Liverpool, London, Norwich and other cities, all held the previous day and all giving vent to lively feelings of anger at the setback to the Bill. Francis Place, in desperation, now played a high-risk tactical game. He had long been known as the back-room mastermind behind all the great political agitations of the early nineteenth century. The son of a debtors' lodging house keeper he had left school at 14 and by his own efforts had become the master tailor of Charing Cross Road known to every history book dealing with the period. It was, of course, the room behind the shop that became so important and the passage to it so well trodden. From it Place directed the campaigns of Sir Francis Burdett when he became the long-sitting member for the turbulent constituency of Westminster. Here too, with Joseph Hume, he plotted and secured the repeal of the Combination Acts which had made trade unions illegal. He was also a close adviser to royalty and a friend of Jeremy Bentham whose utilitarian ideas were to give birth to so many reforms of the Victorian age. He was a masterly tactician and now he was to use his skill to gamble with the future of the Constitution.

Many of the Lords, aided and abetted by Queen Adelaide, whose name was consequently removed from many public-houses, set out to persuade the King to make the Duke of Wellington prime minister and allow him to do what he would, including wreck the Bill. Although the army was only 11,000 strong, Wellington had said in October 1831 that, "the people of England are very quiet if they are let alone, but if they won't be quiet, there is a way to make them." And privately he left his friends in no doubt that he only wanted the opportunity. By May 1832 insurrection was expected. The NPU now held meetings every evening and began to prepare armed resistance to the Duke. Place has recorded that if Wellington had been appointed prime minister there would have been open civil and military response. Soldiers of all ranks, as well as military and naval men of wide experience, were in contact with Place and were ready to organize and conduct the operations of the people. Even generals and colonels were involved. And by now many people were armed with swords, pike-heads and muskets. The clouds of revolution threatened.

On May 12 Place and delegates from many parts of the country held a secret meeting in Covent Garden at which they hit upon the call: "To Stop The Duke, Go for Gold." Apparently sufficient money was raised on the spot to have bill-stickers at work posting the bills in less than four hours. Then they were on their way throughout the land. Place wrote to the government warning that if they let the Duke take office as Premier there would be civil war with the money "at our command." "If we obtain the money," he claimed, "he cannot get it ... we shall have the power to feed and lead the people and in less than five days we shall have the soldiers with us."

Behind the message, which Place hoped would be enough to forestall the appointment, plans went ahead to have towns like Birmingham barricaded, to have families of Tory lords seized and held as hostages for the conduct of the Duke towards reformers and for a call to soldiers to join the people. On May 16, *The Times,* in a leading article, strongly attacked the Duke for preparing coercive laws. Such "oppressive and revolting laws *must* be enforced by violence - there is no other method. It is not then the people's Bill, but the people's butchery!" Claiming that there would be reform or revolution the paper asserted: "The Tories do not dread the mob: the mob is their natural ally." It considered an armed people embraced the nation itself and would not make war on itself or its representatives. Tory papers were less than enthusiastic, reflecting on the panic afflicting the City at the prospect of the threatened run on gold. As delegates prepared to depart for the country to put their plans into effect the bankers were equally busy behind the scenes and Lord Grey was at last given full powers to carry the Bill.

If the temper of the times gave Place the will to use arms it can be understood how Wakley was so forceful, although, it must be remembered, he never ceased to espouse the rule of law. But Place's gamble paid off. He had wider support than Wakley and the ear of influential members of the government. He had always hoped and prayed his tactics would succeed. Thus he opposed with all his skills of delay the holding of a mass meeting on Hampstead Heath on which members of the NPU had set their hearts. He seems to have anticipated an attendance of half a million and he had the venue changed to Regents Park on May 11, although why that should be safer is not clear, unless he thought the area more respectable and the park more enclosed. He also confided to his journal that the difference between the NPU and NUWC was that the one desired the Reform Bill to prevent a revolution and the other desired its destruction as a means of producing a revolution. However, in the event once again the magician had pulled the trick. The Bill received the Royal Assent on June 7. An historic event coinciding with the death of Jeremy Bentham, Place's mentor.

It is clear that, despite his contingency plans, Place rallied London to put pressure on the government. Yet those "doctrinaire revolutionaries", the Rotundists, had threatened his alliance and caused consternation in the ranks of the Whigs. James Mill, that outstanding theorist of the middle class, had written to Place on October 25, 1831 expressing his concern that a deputation from the working class had filled the editor of the *Morning Chronicle* with alarm. Place, in an effort to calm Mill, retorted that it was not a deputation from the working people but "two out of half-a-dozen who manage, or mismanage, the meetings of the Rotunda in Blackfriars Road."

However, it is significant that the Duke of Wellington saw the essence of the reform struggle as a contest between the establishment and the Rotunda, which he described as two engaged armies. He regretted he could place no river between the armies with adequate sentinels and posts on the bridges because the enemy was installed at sensitive points within his own camp. And John Croker, influential Secretary to the Admiralty, claimed the struggle was no longer between two political parties for the Ministry, but between the mob and the government.

It is a matter of conjecture what would have happened if Wakley and other Rotunda leaders had not been kept out of the leadership of the NPU by Place. It is extremely unlikely that, despite all the talk of revolution, the country would have taken that path. In any event, Wakley and his friends wanted not revolution but more widespread and effective reforms. Nevertheless, the situation was extremely volatile and if Wellington had carried out his threat to use the army, the consequences would have been incalculable. In that context the importance of the support Place and his colleagues were able to rally to the government cannot be overestimated. On the other hand could a more militant NPU have secured amendments to the Bill more favourable to the working class? It is doubtful in the extreme. The Whigs desired working-class support, but were quite unwilling to share power as the price for it. It remains impossible to determine what the sequel would have been. History books do not mention Wakley's highly articulate role in this episode, possibly because he did not succeed. Perhaps, also, it is disconcerting to contemplate what might have happened if he had. Yet, a careful reading of what Wakley said and did at the time does not indicate that he was the violent revolutionary of Place's imagination. In fact he was genuinely concerned at what he saw as a gigantic trick being played on the working class in which later historians, without mentioning him, have shown he was right. In that sense he was a visionary ahead of his time.

It is known that, apart from the activities already mentioned, Wakley spoke frequently at the Rotunda meetings which were held as regularly as three times a week during the height of the reform agitation. Although a freelance Rotundist, he often took the chair and repeatedly gained prolonged applause when he objected that the Bill failed to provide for the participation in Parliament of the wealth producers and, indeed, reduced their role in elections by depriving scot-and-lot electors in the boroughs of votes they already had. And Captain Swing, he would say in jocular vein, when he discovered he had no rights conferred on him by the Bill, would burn with indignation!

During the whole period, with his usual indefatigable energy, Wakley had also produced his own weekly newspaper, *The Ballot*. Remarkably like *The Times* in size and appearance, and with front page advertisements, the first number rolled off the presses on Sunday, January 2, 1831. Its price, 7d. Typically, from its second issue it bore beneath its name the legend: "Edited by Thomas Wakley - to avoid the charge of 'secret' writing." Its first leader stated in uncomprising tones that the paper's title declared in one word its political creed and that it would be independent and impartial in attacks on Tory and Whig boroughmongers until corruption was destroyed. It was an advanced position to take at the time but, as always, Wakley remembered the general reader whom he wished to reach. *The Ballot* was to be a newspaper, not a journal to be read by a few of the converted. It contained news, reports from coroners and law courts, theatre notices, foreign intelligence, parliamentary proceedings, political articles about France, unjust trials and so on. In true Wakley style there was also a regular column headed, "Lies par excellence" and quotes from other newspapers that were patently untrue.

By September 1831 there were frequently strong leaders

urging the case for the Reform Bill. On October 9 the paper gave a long analytical report of the House of Lords debates of the Bill on October 3 and 7 and when the Lords defeated the Bill after it had passed the Commons, the *Ballot* appeared on the streets with black lines bordering each column. Wakley called on the people to remain calm, to support Grey and Brougham as pilots who would still safely guide the Bill on to the statute book, and to petition the King to create new peers to provide a majority for the Bill. So cogent was this appeal that it was reprinted as a handbill by an independent publisher and widely circulated as a "heart-stirring appeal to the people of Great Britain." All of which is, of course, a far cry from Place categorizing Wakley as being opposed to the Bill in the name of instant revolution.

The paper also gave blow-by-blow accounts of the reaction in the country and under the rubric "Victims of the Odious Six Acts" gave the names of those sentenced, the length of sentence and the prisons in which they were incarcerated. And a subscription was opened to help their families in the absence of any other relief.

Following the Bristol riots the paper reported the NPU meeting at the Crown & Anchor and a NUWC meeting on November 4 where, it stated, Wakley had declared that he "felt a great interest in the welfare of the working classes - he had from his boyhood." He said he had accepted the chair for the forthcoming open-air meeting on November 7 to enforce peace, and had called upon members not to attend with staves. However, he had now seen Lord Melbourne who, following the violent attack on the Recorder of Bristol, had threatened to arrest those at the meeting for an overt act of treason. He, therefore, urged that the meeting be postponed and was supported by Watson, Lovett and Cleave who said they feared provocateurs would attend to create another Bristol. After Wakley's defeat at the NPU meeting already referred to, he showed better grace and more political understanding than the prejudiced Place by penning a leader in the *Ballot* calling upon people to support the NPU and help bring about a union of the middle and working classes.

When Grey was restored to office in May 1832 to finally enact the Reform Bill, Wakley jubilantly poured bitter scorn on Wellington, the defeated hero. "Alas, Dukey", he wrote, "where art thou? Discomforted old man, go thy ways ... what a pitiful picture does this conqueror of armies and of states present of fallen greatness! - not of *real* greatness, but of that species of 'glory' arising from the hue reflected by sacrifices of human blood. Wellington fought not for freedom, risked not his life for the liberties and happiness of his countrymen, but for the success of the hellish designs of the Holy Alliance - for perpetuating the misrule of the boroughmongers."

A week later, after Place had declared the NUWC an illegal body when faced with a motion to admit its members to a meeting of the NPU, Wakley called Lord Chancellor Brougham's insistence that the Bill was a "final measure" preposterous, since the working class needed to be enfranchised. Nevertheless, on June 10, 1832, the *Ballot* proclaimed that the Bill was now the People's Act of Parliament despite Wakley seeing that its vital weakness was that the secret ballot had not been achieved and the working people were still without representation.

And now, different times - different methods. He wound up the paper on November 4, although not before he had sent a letter dated October 30 to the electors of Finsbury declaring, in reply to a deputation, his willingness to stand for Parliament. He wanted no misunderstandings, however, and set out in no uncertain terms his opinions on the issues of the ballot, military flogging, triennial Parliaments, the restoration of the scot-and-lot right of voting, the repeal of the Corn Laws and of primogeniture, the abolition of tithes and stamp duties on newspapers and reform of the law including abolition of the death penalty. It was a political manifesto to do credit to any liberal mind of the 1830s. It is clear he saw his tasks as a future MP as far wider than that of member for medicine as claimed by his official biographer and others. He was, in truth, a genuine early democrat and not, as some of his modern critics have claimed, a sham humanitarian.

Yet even after the Reform Bill had been enacted and the dust had settled Place could not forgive Wakley. In his Journals he first describes him as a tall, stout man with fair hair and a rather florid complexion who was a remarkably good speaker. And then comes the venom. "One of the most vehement ill-judging of men Mr. (sic) Thomas Wakley, proprietor of the Lancet Medical Journal and the Ballot newspaper, was advertised as the chairman ... To the disgrace of the Borough of Finsbury this man was at the last election returned as their representative in Parliament." This last was an error for at the time about which Place was writing Wakley was not yet elected and it is curious since much of the content of the Journals is based on contemporaneous papers and records. The mistake is repeated by Place's biographer, Graham Wallas, although Wakley was not elected to the House of Commons until 1835. It is also surprising that Dr. C.W. Brook, a great admirer of Wakley, has written that in 1832 Place encouraged Wakley to stand for Parliament. Nothing seems more unlikely. But it may be accounted for by the fact that Brook, like Sprigge before him, could write about Wakley's life and not mention his role in the Reform Bill agitation.

For good measure Place went on to describe Wakley as having a somewhat swaggering air, a suspicious cast of countenance and added that he "would be a formidable fellow were he not as all such men are in most particulars a coward - physically and morally." This was completely untrue but perhaps Place is not too much to be blamed for allowing his imagination to run riot since Wakley was probably the most formidable opponent he ever encountered on his own side. Whilst Place's upbringing led him to support reform, Wakley was from a different background and surprisingly had a deeper and wider interest in the poor and their future.

It was an explosive episode in Wakley's life in which he espoused principles he was never to sacrifice even when later he became less strident in expressing them. He never lost his inspiration to work for the interests of the working class and of the oppressed and weak generally. Equally, his belief in democracy never faltered.

Such principles also explain Wakley's later assistance in formulating the aims of the Chartists, who were in direct descent from the Rotundists, as well as his vivid advocacy in the House of Commons on behalf of the Tolpuddle Martyrs. It was, in fact, a side effect of the enactment of the Reform Bill that enabled Cobbett to be elected as MP for Oldham in 1832 and Wakley for Finsbury in 1835.

The Dead-Body Bill

Whilst all this agitation was proceeding Wakley was also active through the columns of the *Lancet,* which Place said he used to alarm the people, to obtain improvements in a Bill to Regulate Schools of Anatomy, popularly known as the "dead-body Bill". The subject had been unsuccessfully tackled earlier when the Earl of Harewood had argued successfully that Parliament could legislate for the living but not the dead. By 1831, however, scare stories were so prevalent after the Burke and Hare murders that many people were afraid to venture out in the dark in London. There was a widespread and growing fear of being murdered and of having the body sold to the surgeons. A large number of newspapers made things worse with sensational copy, especially the *Morning Herald* which was dubbed, "the representative of the ignorance of the people." Speedily there emerged a bitter hatred of the "human carcass butchers", as the surgeons were called, and all in any way concerned in anatomical studies.

Wakley thought the prejudice arose from using the bodies of murderers and what he described as the disgusting and filthy practice of illegal exhumation. He saw the Bill as inefficient and, in so far as it authorized the sale of bodies, likely to promote "Burking". Never, he said, would he concur in a Bill which permitted the sale of dead bodies and dealing in human flesh and bones. Otherwise the Bill would prove not only worthless but highly injurious. The required certificate of death he thought laughable since if a man would commit murder he was unlikely to stop at forgery. He said the promoter of the Bill, Warburton, meant well but he should seize the bull by the horns and not by the tail, where he might be three parts kicked to death. He then called upon the profession to petition Parliament for the enactment of a law to render the buying or selling of a dead human body an offence. However, some bodies were essential for medical science and he favoured a policy of free voluntary bequest but did not oppose using bodies of unclaimed paupers of which there was a plentiful supply.

As we have seen the grave-snatching trade was destroyed with the Anatomy Act of 1832 which permitted the use only of "unclaimed" workhouse bodies, provided an inspector certified the cause of death, and even then solely in schools of anatomy licensed under the Act. Wakley failed to secure all the amendments in the Bill he desired, but undoubtedly contributed to the general improvement of the law.[1]

---

1. For a full examination of how the Act "criminalized" the poor see the excellent study, *Death, Dissection and the Destitute* by Ruth Richardson (Routledge & Kegan Paul) 1987.

CHAPTER 5

CRUSADING RADICAL

It may seem somewhat ironic that the Wakley of the Rotunda should wish to sit in the House of Commons. However, it was a reformed Parliament despite falling far short of what Wakley had desired and, indeed, Finsbury was one of its new constituencies. Furthermore, he might well have considered it the best arena in which to wage future struggles for his political objectives, and there was always his acute interest in medical legislation. After all, the air was full of plans for the reform of well-nigh everything and with Benthamite fervour numerous Royal Commissions and Select Committees were being appointed to consider change on a bewildering number of issues. It was as if reform mania had gripped the country. If then these were his reasons he was to prove them justified beyond expectation.

In 1826, with *The Lancet* a success financially, Wakley had moved his home to 35 Bedford Square, WC1, where there is now a plaque to commemorate his long stay. It was a double-fronted Georgian residence with its entrance enhanced, as was the fashion, with a tasteful semi-circular fanlight. Another important feature was its Adam ceiling which graced the front drawing room on the first floor. The building remains impressive today, housing a fine library and architectural exhibitions. Here his ambition to enter the House of Commons gradually matured. He became well known locally with his profuse hospitality at home and, more importantly, by his energetic campaigning on the burning issue of the enormous rates with which his future constituents were saddled. Also he was an Anglican and active churchwarden. To this must be added his well-earned fame as editor of *The Lancet.* What is more, he had long proposed in *The Lancet,* for reasons which will be discussed later, that Coroners should be medical men and not lawyers. Consequently, when in 1830 he stood as the first medical candidate for Coroner of East Middlesex, his name was again public property and aroused intense interest. Over 400 freeholders were present at his first meeting in the campaign, held at the Crown & Anchor tavern in the Strand. There the atmosphere soon became warm with support for Wakley, not only as a doctor, but as a man who could defeat lawyers even in their own courts.

It so happened that this was the same week in which Wakley secured a verdict of manslaughter against a notorious charlatan by the name of John St. John Long. The origin of the case lay in a distressing tragedy. Long, who was born in poor circumstances, was a remarkable man. After starting work in Limerick as a portrait painter he migrated to London and, with a slight knowledge of anatomy and a liniment, set up as a medical saviour of mankind. This ointment, he claimed, not only cured diseases but also revealed them. His practice was to place a few drops of a vitriolic liquid on the skin which would speedily produce ulceration. He then applied the ointment to keep the sore open for as long as he required to extract sufficient fees from the patient. Long cultivated society and would prophesy deaths of healthy people to their relatives or friends and be rewarded with the "patients" coming to him in droves. It was calculated by the *Gentleman's Magazine* that in one year alone he acquired a sum of £13,400 in fees - a huge sum for the time. Here then was just the sort of quack against whom Wakley had campaigned so vigorously.

The torture of these imaginary invalids went on for some years until a catastrophe occurred in the summer of 1830 which aroused the anger of the nation. Two sisters named Cashin approached Long for treatment of the younger, who was in poor health. Long prescribed a mild inhalant for the sick girl and then turned his sights on the healthy sister. He told the girls' mother on August 2 that unless the elder sister underwent treatment with his liniment she would rapidly become a consumptive. The mother consented and after 10 days of agony the girl was suffering extreme pain and had become seriously ill. An enormous ulcer had been produced on her back and she was vomiting continually. The following day Long assured her she would soon be in perfect health, but by August 17, only two weeks after the "treatment" commenced, she was dead, aged 24.

Wakley used *The Lancet* to publicize the case throughout the land. Approached by relatives of the unfortunate girl to attend the inquest on their behalf he at first refused. He said that having publicized the case he might appear biased and that as a candidate for coroner he could be accused of advertising himself. However, the family having no friends in London, and knowing of Long's influence in society, would not be denied. So Wakley agreed to represent them before the coroner and Mr. Adolphus QC, who we have seen as one of the defence counsel for the Cato Street conspirators and Wakley in his arson trial, acted on behalf of Long. Adolphus tried to persuade the jury that the medical profession was jealous of Long and that the girl's resistance to Long's healing treatment, and therefore her death, had resulted from relieving her feverish thirst with plums. Wakley, for his part, drew on the facts to demonstrate that Long had killed a perfectly healthy young woman, and he secured a verdict of manslaughter.

Dr. James Johnson, whom Wakley had once sued for libel for calling him Lucifer, promptly congratulated him in the *Medico-Chirurgical Review* and wrote of his forensic conflict with Adolphus:

Wakley was opposed to a lawyer whose practice at the Old Bailey and engagement in cases declined by the respectable members of the Bar rendered him capable of using all kinds of mean artifices and personal insults for the purpose of browbeating his antagonist. Yet Mr. Wakley set him down repeatedly, and that by coolness of temper and strength of argument. Galled and foiled and irritated to a fury by a medical man uneducated to the Bar, and whom he hoped to crush by his Newgate ribaldry, he at length appealed to the coroner to prevent Mr. Wakley from opposing him at all.

The account rings true but from Johnson has to be treated with caution.

All this, of course, improved Wakley's chance of being elected coroner for East Middlesex. Large meetings were held in his support in Islington and Clerkenwell where he was received with great enthusiasm. Nevertheless, only freeholders were entitled to vote and the idea of a medical coroner was entirely innovative. In the result Wakley was defeated by a solicitor, but only by a small margin of 136 out of poll of 7,204. And the ability and eloquence he revealed in this election were a direct cause of his being requested to stand for Parliament in Finsbury two years later.

To complete the story of Long; in consequence of the verdict of the coroner's jury he was arraigned at the Old Bailey on October 30, when counsel for the Crown adopted Wakley's line of approach. Long's counsel put in the witness box a marquis, a marchioness and her daughters, and the heir to one of the most ancient earldoms in the land, all of whom testified to their faith in Long's treatment. Despite this display of aristocratic support the jury found Long guilty, but the Judge was more impressed. It seems almost inconceivable today that Mr. Justice Parke fined him a trifling £250, which he drew from his pocket and paid on the spot. Perhaps it had something to do with the fact that one of the witnesses for the defence sat with the Judge and talked to him during much of the trial. At least the leniency of the sentence produced a public outcry which was increased when a second of Long's victims perished. Another coroner's jury produced another verdict of manslaughter and a further trial at the Old Bailey ensued when the Judge allowed him to go free on the ground that the medical evidence against him was too weak.

Sensibility to human suffering and loss of life must have been much lower in the medical profession at that time since, incredible as it may seem, a Dr. Francis Ramadge decided to spring to Long's defence. Ramadge was a Doctor of Medicine at Oxford University and a Fellow of the Royal College of Physicians yet he wrote an ingratiating letter to the totally unqualified Long who, not surprisingly, immediately had it published in *The Sunday Times.* Such publication revealed that Ramadge had denigrated his fellow doctors who had given evidence against Long at his trials, praised Long's treatment of his two dead patients and expressed regret at the "unmerited" contempt with which he now found himself surrounded.

Wakley republished the letter in *The Lancet,* argued questions of law arising from the case and called upon Ramadge to retire from the profession. Immediately Ramadge was expelled from the Medical Society of London of which he was a member. Wakley followed this by publishing the details when, a few weeks later, another doctor refused to meet Ramadge at a patient's bedside, a refusal which the patient endorsed. Ramadge promptly sued Wakley for libel. Wakley defended himself and described Long, who was in court, as a quack and a felon. No libel writ could follow that remark'which was protected by privilege. He further claimed that to hold Ramadge up to contempt was the only course open to an honest medical writer. After only a few minutes' deliberation the jury contemptuously awarded Ramadge damages of one farthing. As for Long he died on July 2, 1834, aged 37, from the ravages of pulmonary tuberculosis, the disease he claimed to cure.

As a postscript, on August 23, *The Lancet* carried the

following announcement: "As that arch-imposter John Long has ceased to live, a worthy votary of his living at Camden Town has advertised that he is in possession of Long's 'secret'. If the nobility should nibble at a bait like this, they are lost past redemption. It is our duty to tell this simple advertiser that the 'secret' of every knave is dishonesty."

Election in Finsbury

The first General Election after the enactment of the Reform Act was held in December 1832. Wakley was by now highly popular in his home constituency of Finsbury and when 600 prominent electors there invited him to be a candidate he agreed to stand as an independent Radical. True to his Rotunda background he would not join the Whigs whom he considered had betrayed the working class after using their assistance to achieve what the Chartist leader and historian, R.C. Gammage, called the "Charter of the Middle Class". Even Daniel O'Connell, who remained an ally of the Whigs, was provoked by their Irish Coercion Bill into denouncing them as "the base, brutal, and bloody Whigs". So, Wakley's inclination for democracy drew him towards the small radical group of MPs, including J.A. Roebuck, Joseph Hume and Dr. Bowring, whilst retaining his independence. He declared himself in favour of a further extension of the suffrage, of triennial elections, of removal of property qualifications from candidates, of the repeal of the Corn Laws, of the abolition of slavery and of the suspension of stamp duty on newspapers. At the time Finsbury was a new two-member constituency which extended from the notorious Seven Dials in Holborn to Stoke Newington in the North East. It had a population of 330,000, of whom 16,000 had the vote. It embraced City Road, off which there is now a street named after Wakley. He was encouraged by Joseph Hume and William

Cobbett, and the 600 ratepayers who invited him to stand constituted themselves an election committee. In addition to his formal declaration of aims he let it be known that he believed electors had the right to compel an MP to abide by his election promises and that he favoured an overhaul of legal procedure to help poor litigants. However, to save expense he took no part in the campaign except to address meetings. In fact, George Rogers, a popular tradesman locally, ran the campaign at a total cost of only £50 which included certain mandatory payments. In the result the Tories were successful with Robert Grant already an MP for 14 years, securing 4,278 votes and Serjeant Spankie, a prominent barrister, 2,848. Wakley came fourth with 2,151.

In 1834 Grant was appointed Governor of Bombay and a by-election was called. Wakley stood again but this time his main opponent was Thomas Duncombe, another Radical. Duncombe was a strange mixture. An aristocrat, a beau and a wit, he was also a specialist in foreign affairs and destined to be the parliamentary spokesman of the Chartists. However, he was described by Greville as a "doubtful character, whose life had been spent on the racecourse and in the green-room, of limited capacity, exceedingly ignorant, and without any stock but his imprudence to trade on."

To keep the Tory out both Radicals agreed that whoever polled the least votes on the first day (at the time polling was conducted over several days) would stand down and urge his supporters to vote for the other. Under this friendly arrangement Wakley withdrew on the second day and Duncombe was successful. This reflected a turning of the tide against the Tories in Finsbury and in the General Election held in January 1835 the electors went Radical and returned Duncombe with 4,497 votes and Wakley with 3,359. A threat to split Wakley's vote by Henry Hobhouse, another Radical, was defeated with Hobhouse obtaining only 1,817 votes. Thus, despite Greville's strictures, began a political partnership which was to last 17 years until Wakley retired from the House of Commons.

Wakley's supporters could hardly contain their enthusiasm at the result. His horses were taken from his carriage on Islington Green and he was dragged home in triumph. There the crowd insisted on hearing him repeatedly from the balcony of his drawing room. Over 10,000 people filled the square, where the railings were pulled up and considerable damage done, with the celebration continuing to a very late hour. So large a crowd had been drawn not only by Wakley's platform, popular though it was, but also by his lively style of oratory and his frequent use of mimicry and invective. Something of his magnetism for a volatile electorate can be gauged even from the descriptions of him by his opponents. "... honest as he is fearless and determined; - a man who would crush an enemy as he would a wasp," wrote Dr. Robert Willis, a rival medical editor. "... a Nasmyth's hammer, he could smooth a curl or crack a pate with equal facility," wrote Sir John Forbes, another rival editor. "The power of the man was apparent ere even a word was spoken" and "resentful of all narrow abuses" are other typical examples.

As for his platform, on the three great issues dominating the politics of the day Wakley had campaigned to support Free Trade, most of the future demands of the Chartists, and repeal of the Act of Union with Ireland. Furthermore, as the ill-effects of the Poor Law Amendment Act came to light he quickly took up the cudgels against them. The first issue, it may be added, brought him into sharp conflict with his land-owning father.

The Tolpuddle Martyrs

Despite the differences with his father Wakley's upbringing in

Devon and on the borders of Dorset made him well qualified to champion the cause of the Tolpuddle Martyrs which first revealed to the House of Commons that they now had in their midst one of the ablest orators of the day. Six agricultural labourers in the small Dorset village of Tolpuddle had been arrested in 1834 for swearing men into a lodge which was intended to join Robert Owen's Grand National Consolidated Trade Union, and the objects of which deplored violence. They had not even threatened a strike. They merely combined to resist a reduction in their wages from nine shillings a week in 1830 to six. Yet the full power of the state using the Mutiny Act of 1797 was brought to bear upon them.

On March 19, 1834 they were convicted at Dorchester Assizes and all sentenced by Mr. Baron Williams to seven years' transportation. There can be no doubt that they were not guilty as charged. Indeed, according to George Lovelace in his *The Victims of Whiggery* (1837) "... the Judge told us that not for anything we had done, or, as he could prove, we intended to do, but or an example to others, he considered it his duty to pass the sentence of seven years' transportation ..." Had they been tried by magistrates in the normal way for belonging to an unlawful combination under the Unlawful Societies Act, 1799, the maximum sentence would have been three months. The nation was stunned and the sentence finally alienated the working class from the Whig government. Whilst they languished in the decaying hulks at Portsmouth awaiting transportation, more than 30,000 people led, amongst others, by Wakley joined a vast demonstration in Copenhagen Fields, King's Cross to protest against the savage sentences. Troops and 5,000 special constables were hastily brought in but the meeting was peaceful, although a petition taken to Home Secretary, Lord Melbourne, was rejected.

By May 27, 1835 Wakley was in a position to present to the House 16 petitions with over 13,000 signatures for the reprieve of the convicts. According to Joseph Hume, speaking in the House, over 800,000 had signed such petitions. Wakley made a short speech in which he disclosed that the wives and families of the men had not only been reduced to poverty but had even been refused parish relief. He gave notice that in one month's time he would move a resolution that the sentences should be annulled. On June 25, Lord John Russell, the Home Secretary, requested Wakley to postpone his motion since the government had already recommended a partial remission of the sentences. He was supported by the Member for Dorset. To Wakley that was not sufficient to satisfy justice, particularly as it was conditional on the men remaining in Australia for some time and the Lovelaces, whom Russell called "the greater criminals", for ever. Russell also urged Wakley not to press a motion of "so unusual a character, interfering as it necessarily must with the prerogative of the Crown." Wakley then rose in a crowded House and at once expressed his astonishment that the Member for Dorset, who had been the foreman of the Grand Jury, should intervene between the sufferers and the seat of mercy (i.e. the House).

He then gave details of the circumstances under which the men had been prosecuted and of the biased charge delivered by the Judge to the Grand Jury of the county in which he wrongly implied all secret societies were illegal. He called the attention of the House to the Act of 1824 which provided that workmen might legally combine to any extent, and in any form they pleased, with respect to the trades in which they were engaged without subjecting themselves to any legal sanction. In particular, it provided that nothing in the Act should subject any persons to punishment for meeting to consult upon the rate of wages. The combination of the six men was merely to protect themselves; they had notice of the latest reduction in their wages, from seven shillings to six shillings, and desired only to save themselves and their families from a diminution in their scanty earnings, which was to them nothing less than starvation. The union of the labourers was legal he declared and the Act under which they were punished for administering unlawful oaths did not apply to their case. Indeed, it would mean numerous Orange Lodges in England were illegal societies. He had consulted almost half the barristers in the House and none could tell him under what precise law those men were condemned, or could say that the conviction or indeed the prosecution was legal. He therefore appealed to the Home Secretary to revoke the sentences imposed on the unfortunate men.

He then proceeded to outline to the House the character and conduct of the men, especially of those who had been received into the Wesleyan Conference as preachers. As they had attracted large congregations he feared very much that that was their great offence. He also considered that there was something behind the scenes which would not, but which ought to, come out. He blushed for the character of his country, he said, while he related the particulars of such a barbarous transaction. He quoted at length from a compassionate letter which had been written from the Hulks by George Lovelace to his wife. "Was it fitting, was it just, that such a man as this, for a doubtful offence should be torn from his loved family, and expatriated for the lengthened period of seven years? ... It was enough to drive the working millions into madness and revenge. And hear it", he continued, "Ye Gentlemen of England, who are husbands, and fathers, and brothers - who have wives and children of your own - one woman - ah! poor creature, how painfully is she figured in my mind at this moment - having a husband and six children, and taken from her, her two brothers, her husband, and her eldest son, all at 'one fell swoop', and this, my Lord [addressing Lord John Russell], is your boasted England! This is your country of equal laws and equal justice." He appealed to Russell to extend justice and mercy to those individuals; and if they were allowed to return home, he said he would himself give personal and pecuniary security for the good behaviour of the two Lovelaces.

He implored the House to take this fitting opportunity of extending mercy to the men, thereby gratifying thousands of the labouring classes who had appeared before the House as petitioners. His prayer to the House was for the restoration of all the prisoners to their families. He beseeched them to concede the favour - to gratify the humane wishes of the working people of England, who had implored the House for mercy for their fellow-labourers. The people of England, he assured the House, felt deeply on the subject. To the working classes especially it was a constant subject of agitation, and unless the men were restored, that agitation would continually increase. The society was legal with the single exception of the oath; and when the object was legal, the oath alone could not make the society illegal. In any event the oath could have been dealt with by magistrates. The prosecution was an unmitigated act of tyrrany. He hoped the House would interpose its authority; it was nothing to say there was no precedent; let them make one as soon as they could, for as it had been well said the night before that they did not need one to do right. He had no object in bringing forward the Motion, but the interests of the working classes. He regretted that the labouring classes had no representatives in the House. He trusted there would be no misinterpretation of his motives; he had entered the Motion a month before, in hope that the men would be restored without his bringing it forward, and that entering the Motion on the books would lead to investigation, and that investigation would lead to a conviction that the men had committed no offence whatever in a moral point of view. He therefore moved for a full pardon for the six Dorchester Labourers.

Wakley's speech lasted two and a half hours. It was regarded by both supporters and opponents alike as a great triumph and when he sat down he received unrestrained applause. The Motion was seconded by Joseph Hume, but was opposed by Lord John Russell for the Whig government and by Sir Robert Peel for the opposition. Daniel O'Connell said the speech had produced an effect such as he had never seen exceeded in his life, but claiming he knew from bitter experience that the applause would not be translated into votes he urged Wakley to withdraw the Motion. With a better tactical sense than even the great O'Connell he again refused and in his reply to the debate disposed of Russell's claim that the Motion interfered with the prerogative of the Crown. He pointed to examples of earlier "interference" by the House, adding that they had as much a duty to address the Crown as to address Ministers if they thought punishment undeserved. "They were", he quoted, "the great council of the nation: Ministers were merely the council of the Prince." Despite all his passion and eloquence the Motion received 82 votes with 308 against.

Yet Wakley had not only spoken from the heart, he had also presented a strong legal case against the convictions as a perusal of the full speech reveals. In consequence the speech and the vote made a deep impression in the country and his efforts eventually prevailed. As he had predicted, the agitation continued unabated and on March 19, 1836, he drew from Lord John Russell a statement that the six men had received a free pardon and were to be immediately returned from Australia at the government's expense. Proof, Wakley called it, of the sovereignty of the people.

Just how advanced Wakley's position on the Martyrs was can be seen by comparing his unequivocal stand with the attitudes of liberals like Russell and Brougham. Whatever Russell's private view was, publicly he made no move without pressure from inside and outside the House of Commons. And Brougham used his skilful oratory, and his prestige as Lord Chancellor, actually to attack the Tolpuddle victims. "It was," he said, "the most audacious assessment, the most foul and unpardonable calumny against the Judges of the country and the laws of the land, to assert that the six men had been sentenced and punished because they were members of a trade union. They had been tried and convicted, and were now suffering punishment for one of the worst offences that could be conceived. The administering of secret oaths was an offence most dangerous in itself, fraught with worse dangers still, leading to the violation of the rights of property, even to assassination itself." Not for Wakley such sophistry. Although today Wakley's role in the campaign to free the convicts goes largely unremarked it was not so at the time. On April 25, 1836, a public dinner of thanksgiving was held at White Conduit House. Nearly 2,000 people attended and Wakley, who presided, was enthusiastically feted. A picture of the poster proclaiming the dinner now fittingly hangs in the T.U.C. Memorial Museum in the village of Tolpuddle.

Just prior to the dinner Wakley had moved in the House on March 8 that leave be granted to bring in a Bill to provide for proper payment to medical witnesses at inquests. Post-mortems, he pointed out, could take as long as eight to 10 hours and it was important that they should not be conducted in haste. Yet the coroner had no authority to re-imburse the medical men and consequently had no power to order an autopsy without which a jury could not reach a correct verdict. The office of coroner was the only office to which the people of England still had the right to elect their own Judge. But unless he could compensate medical witnesses the court had a tendency to become almost useless. He referred to an inquest held a few days earlier at Woolwich barracks where a marine had died after being flogged. From medical evidence the jury had reached the conclusion that a terrible outrage had been committed, but if the medical men had been mercenary enough not to attend, an injustice would have resulted. Sir John

Campbell, the Attorney-General, and Sir R. Rolfe, the Solicitor-General, supported Wakley but there was some opposition. Nevertheless, leave was given to bring in the Bill and within three months it became law. The medical profession secured payment for professional services and the public acquired additional security against the risks of undetected murder. Wakley's reputation was now assured.

Prisoners' Counsel

As will be seen Wakley had a particular hatred of lawyers and their "closed shop" mentality, associated with his dislike of the medical oligarchy. This led to a curious incident during the passage through the Commons of the Prisoners' Counsel Bill in 1836. At the time prisoners accused of felony were not permitted to have counsel address the jury on their behalf even though death was the penalty for most crimes including many of a trivial nature. The Bill was intended to remedy that situation. Its acceptance was by no means a foregone conclusion, however, since such a measure had been fought for by law reformers for over a decade and had always foundered on opposition from lawyers in the Commons and by the House of Lords. Somewhat mischievously Wakley proposed in Committee an Amendment to the Bill to grant prisoners the right to be defended by anyone, not merely counsel. Both counsel and attornies (solicitors), he said, belonged to "self-constituted and arbitrary societies, who really were not themselves amenable to law in their regulations."

Rather surprisingly, in light of the danger it presented to the Bill's acceptance, its mover William Ewart, another advanced radical, supported the idea although he thought the attempt hopeless. Other friends of Wakley's including Daniel O'Connell, saw a clear danger to a progressive measure and called upon him to withdraw the amendment. Undoubtedly if it had been accepted the passage of the Bill would have been blocked. There was little fear it would be agreed, however, and the Attorney-General, Sir John Campbell, helped secure its defeat, arguing that it would open the door for any returned convict from Botany Bay to put on a wig and gown and appear as the advocate of a prisoner on his trial. Wakley, of course, would not have required even the wig and gown. However, he did say later that all he had really wanted was an opportunity for prisoners to choose either counsel or an attorney in all trials as the Bill permitted them to do on summary trial before magistrates.

The Bill was finally enacted without the amendment and, in the words of Sir John Campbell in the debate, vindicated the law of England from a "deep and disgraceful stain". This was not achieved, however, until there had taken place a conference between the House of Commons and the House of Lords when the Commons conceded a clause which would have given defence counsel the right of final reply which they have today. Wakley's episode led to the *Annual Register* claiming that the Member for Finsbury had attained popular favour "... by professing all opinions which co-incide with the selfishness, self-conceit and love of power of those who are numerous enough to be called the people, but who make no pretensions to the knowledge and wisdom which should belong to those by whom a people ought to be governed." This nonsense was, however, a predictable response to Wakley's intransigent radicalism.

In May 1836 he was also found opposing the extension of Sunday closing proposed in Sir Andrew Agnew's Sabbath Observance Bill. He made a spirited attack on the narrow view that it was wicked to delight the eye and instruct the mind on the seventh day as "only another of the Lydia heads of cant, sham, hypocrisy, privilege and monopoly." Instead, he urged that the British Museum, as well as other museums, galleries and zoos, should be open on days when workmen could visit them such as holidays and Sundays.

Wakley was also active in endeavouring to secure the abolition of the notorious stamp duties on newspapers, widely regarded as a tax on knowledge. Not only was there a tax on advertisements but each copy of a paper bore a tax of four pence - a considerable sum at the time aimed at inhibiting the publication of cheap popular newspapers. In his usual polemical style Wakley published a pamphlet on April 11, 1836 entitled: "A Letter to the People of England, on the New Project for Gagging the Press." The government had introduced a Bill to consolidate and amend the law which included pamphlets in the definition of a newspaper. Wakley saw the Bill as a "newly fabricated instrument of oppression". Certain clauses were tyrannical, odious, infamous. We are on the point, he exclaimed, of "determining whether there shall, or shall not, be a free press in this country." Is the political press, he queried, to be "chained to Somerset House under the delicate guardianship of a set of censors, or licensers, nicknamed 'Commissioners of Stamps' ...?"

Wakley was concerned at the speed with which the government was pressing the Bill. "My experience in the House of Commons tells me", he wrote, "that bad measures are gifted with an extraordinary celerity of motion in their passage through the two Houses of Parliament". He called upon his readers to let their MPs know their feelings and pointed out that he had presented 30 petitions and joined a deputation of MPs and others to Prime Minister Lord Melbourne on the matter. For Wakley the stamp duties were iniquitous and had to be totally removed.

Although unable to secure total abolition, however, Wakley did help secure the Newspaper Stamp Act of 1836, with a material reduction in the duty to a penny or twopence according to size. He was attacked for compromising but responded with full and well-reasoned arguments. At the time three publishers were in prison for publishing papers without the four pence duty, viz: Henry Hetherington, of the *Poor Man's Guardian,* John Cleave, Wakley's ally at the Rotunda, and James Watson.

In February and April of the same year Wakley pleaded in the House of Commons for the entire abolition of flogging in the army. In a debate on the Mutiny Bill he maintained that the savage practice of military flogging frequently caused the death of soldiers and was in effect a penalty of capital punishment for minor acts of insubordination. He then tabled another Motion calling for the repeal of the Septennial Act in fulfilment of his election pledge to do so. He did not favour annual Parliaments but thought a life of seven years too long. He also supported an inquiry into the working of certain provisions in the Poor Law Amendment Act of 1834, that monument to the utilitarian theory of deterrent hardship which was already causing serious suffering to so many people in need of assistance. He was also a frequent supporter of Daniel O'Connell's repeated demands for Irish self-government. All in all 1836 was an eventful year for Wakley's crusading spirit, both inside and outside Parliament.

Re-election

On the death of William IV another General Election was called, as was customary at the time. It was held in July 1837 and Wakley again presented himself before the electors of Finsbury. This time opposition came from an unexpected quarter. George Rogers, who had been the chairman of all Wakley's election committees in previous contests for Parliament and the office of coroner, suddenly opposed Wakley's candidacy. There is no record of his reasons given during the campaign but on November 11, he published a pamphlet described as a "statement of reasons for not having supported Mr. Wakley at the recent Finsbury election."

It was an angry and highly polemical document. Quite ridiculously, and with no regard for truth, it claimed that as an MP Wakley had done literally nothing to carry out his pledges to the voters. Then, more seriously, it alleged Wakley was to receive large sums of money to distribute to his supporters from taxes raised to carry out the provisions of a Metropolitan Improvement Bill (rejected in the event by the House of Lords). Apparently one of the improvements projected by the Bill was to make a wide new street from Oxford Street to Broad Street, St. Giles by pulling down "low brothels and rookeries" in existing labyrinthine streets. Such projects, which succeeded later, were intended to destroy the crowded squalor of areas of crime and decay like St. Giles and Seven Dials. The latter, with seven streets radiating from a central point, being described by Dickens as a "maze of streets, courts, lanes and alleys ... lost in the unwholesome vapour which hangs over the house-tops, and renders the dirty perspective uncertain and confined". Presumably the money was intended as compensation for the owners of such properties.

Wakley was also charged with not having resigned after three years as an MP in accordance with an alleged promise to do so. An allegation presumably based upon his support for triennial Parliaments. And with having told the electors he was very poor prior to splendidly furnishing 35 Bedford Square and adding a carriage and pair, coachman, footman, etc. to his establishment. Yet it will be recalled that Wakley had had his horses taken from his carriage by those same electors on the night of his first being elected to Parliament. There was much more along similar lines and it is difficult to assess Rogers' motives unless he had hoped to have more influence on Wakley in the House than was the case. At all events his venom could have had little effect as Wakley topped the poll with 4,957 votes to 4,895 for Duncombe and 2,470 for the defeated candidate Dudley Perceval, nephew of assassinated Prime Minister Spencer Perceval. That was, incidentally, the largest majority obtained by any candidate at this General Election.

On the first Address to Parliament from the throne by the young Queen Victoria, Wakley, whose audacity knew no bounds, presented a petition from a constituent which he used, in effect, as an Amendment to the Queen's Speech. This first referred to widespread discontent in the country arising from extreme poverty and wretchedness. It then called for universal suffrage and the ballot, the use of Church and Crown lands to reduce the national debt, abolition of the laws of entail and primogeniture, the separation of Church and State and the abolition of the House of Lords.

No doubt Wakley had a hand in framing the petition and in his speech he described himself as a representative of Labour. His action caused a great deal of consternation. In reply to critics he made no apology but caustically conceded that although he agreed in great measure with the petition he did not want to see the Lords abolished. As to the doubts he caused some Members to express on whether petitions to the Commons should in future be permitted at all he said he hoped he would receive no more since the House never took any notice of them. As he no doubt intended, this statement had no effect whatsoever on subsequent petitioners who desired his services! However, his unprecedented Amendment managed to attract 20 votes.

Chartism

There were even more far-reaching consequences to follow from Wakley's courageous Motion. In the debate it aroused, Lord John Russell declared that he could not countenance any attempts to re-open the questions such as universal suffrage and the ballot that had been settled by the Reform Bill. This ill-judged response earned Russell the nickname "Finality Jack" but, more importantly, it caused bewilderment and anger in the manufacturing districts where it was widely believed that the Reform Bill had been enacted only as a first step to wider changes. A conference was quickly called between certain Liberal and Radical MPs, including Wakley, and working-class leaders. Five demands were formulated, viz: (1) universal suffrage, (2) annual Parliaments, (3) payment of MPs, (4) abolition of the property qualification for parliamentary candidates, and (5) vote by ballot. From these beginnings, flowing from Wakley's Amendment and a meeting in the previous February called by the London Working Men's Association, arose the "People's Charter", and the Chartist movement that was to dominate politics for a decade.

It is noteworthy that even before his Rotunda days Wakley was active for the main demands which gave rise to the Chartist agitation. As early as July 11, 1831, he took the chair at a meeting of delegates from all parts of the country who met at Portman Market in London. Two resolutions were carried at the meeting. One was on the Liberty of the Press. The other calling for universal suffrage, annual parliaments, vote by ballot and removal of the property qualification for MPs.

Despite his prominent part in the birth of Chartism Wakley never had any official connexion with the movement. Indeed, he did not support annual Parliaments, and was lukewarm about the official payment of MPs whose income, he thought, should be provided by their constituents if they had no other source. However, when the "great petition" to the House bearing one and a quarter million signatures was presented by Attwood in July 1839 Wakley spoke eloquently in its favour. In terms reminiscent of the Rotunda debates he called upon the working class to join with the middle class in a demand for the petition in order at least to have an effect on "this assembly". With anger, he added that with the House as at present constituted they might as well petition the rock of Gibraltar. Lord John Russell claimed that the plight of the masses was overstated and he refused to believe stories told of the grievances of agricultural labourers in Devon, a county in whose affairs he was involved. Wakley immediately responded with details of the sufferings of "field slaves" in Devon who toiled from sunrise to sunset in all weathers for a paltry wage of seven shillings a week. They then had to sleep in sheds, barns and outhouses in rags.

Disraeli, sitting in his first Parliament and fully alive to the "two nations" and the aspirations of the Chartists, voted for some parts of the petition but the motion was defeated by an overwhelming majority of 237 to 48. Despite the Reform Act the House of Common still had a considerable number of landed members. In fact they found it easier to get into Parliament after 1832 than before and in the Parliament of 1841-47 out of the 815 who sat in it throughout its length as many as 234 were included in Burke's *Landed Gentry.* Despite the defeat Wakley continued his efforts on behalf of the Chartists, particularly those imprisoned whom he described as political prisoners. These included Feargus O'Connor, the uncrowned king of the Chartists, in York Castle and Henry Vincent in Millbank. And when Duncombe moved for a full inquiry into the harsh conditions of imprisonment of two other Chartist leaders, Wakley seconded the Motion and Disraeli supported, although it could only muster 27 other supporters. He also called for the return of transported Chartists Frost, Williams and Jones, leaders of the Newport Rising in South Wales. The aim of Frost, a former magistrate, was to release Vincent and other leaders from gaol, but he was charged with treason by levying war against the Queen. Such use of the treason laws as a means of political control had a long history and was disliked by juries who in this case made a strong recommendation for mercy. As a result the death sentence was reduced to transportation.

Wakley considered Frost was really involved in an unlawful assembly and riot.

Nevertheless, Wakley always opposed the "physical force" arm of the movement in the belief that its actions were counter-productive. Wakley still opposed the Establishment and supported the working class as firmly as ever, but for him all action had to be undertaken constitutionally and the place for achieving reform was Parliament. He told his electors that whereas lawless rebellion stirred up enmity to good causes among the people, constitutional agitation generally obtained its just demands. Indeed, many Chartist leaders themselves abjured violence and Chartist posters and literature constantly proclaimed the motto of "Peace, Law and Order". Clearly, without distancing himself from mainstream Chartism, he had independently drawn important lessons from the failure of the Rotundists.

Ever-active for trade union victims of unfair trials, on February 13, 1838, Wakley had presented to the House a petition on behalf of five leaders of a strike of Glasgow cotton-spinners who were sentenced to seven years' transportation. The incident which led to the trial had occurred in April 1837 and made a deep impression on the country. Arising out of picketing, the homes of some blacklegs, known locally as "nobs", had been attacked. In one case a "nob" was shot dead. A member of the Cotton Spinners' Association was charged with the murder, and the leaders of the Association with conspiracy to hire him to commit the crime. No complicity in the murder was proved against the leaders but conspiracy was a sufficiently elastic charge for the finding of guilty. Only three years after the Tolpuddle Martyrs the trade union world was again shaken to its foundations. But the effort to blacken trade unionism evoked expressions of working-class solidarity far and wide.

A Select Committee on Combinations of Workmen was formed during 1838 on which Wakley sat. In examining witnesses he established that the employers had given the cotton spinners no increase in wages for nine years prior to the autumn of 1836. An increase awarded then was suddenly withdrawn in April 1837 and the strike was the result. Three weeks later the men returned to work but were told by the masters that they would not be re-engaged unless they took yet a further cut in pay. Wakley made a vigorous speech in the House on behalf of the sentenced leaders and asked the Government not to transport them until there had been a thorough investigation. He followed this by frequently presenting the House with petitions for leniency and the men were ultimately reprieved in July 1840.

In the previous month of June 1840 Sir James Graham's Vaccination Bill was before the Commons. Only the Poor Law medical officers were to be allowed to vaccinate and Wakley opposed this, arguing that each person should be allowed to employ his own medical man. The poor, he said, objected to the proposal, but his amendment was defeated. He effectively won the point with an amendment to another clause, however, and succeeded with a further amendment in making it a criminal offence to inoculate with smallpox, or to intentionally expose people to infection. In the following year Wakley took part in several debates involving medical matters. He strongly supported - albeit unsuccessfully - a measure against burying the dead in overcrowded churchyards in the midst of cities by which he said the dead poisoned the living.

At the time illegitimacy was rising sufficiently rapidly to cause serious alarm. Wakley blamed the misery and distress of the working poor which often prevented marriage. The result was an increase also in infanticide. Wakley wanted legislation against the causes not the consequences. This would involve, he said, general legislation for the working classes, improvement in wages, cheaper food and better sanitary conditions in homes. He also spoke in favour of equal taxation of property and against all sinecures and hereditary pensions. This led to uncomplimentary references to members of the House of Lords although he still did not propose abolition of that Chamber.

Lawyers and Quacks

Many of his speeches also made disdainful references to lawyers and the legal profession. Wakley was successful in most of his legal actions, and undoubtedly would have made a brilliant lawyer himself, but he held to a passionate dislike of the legal profession throughout his life. The origin of this hatred is difficult to trace. It may relate to experiences with lawyers in his many cases although he always remained on friendly terms with Brougham, who acted for him in his early trials. More likely it arose from his strong aversion to monopoly, greed and hypocrisy which he exposed in the medical profession and no doubt discerned in the legal profession. At the time both professions were overmanned and, for most practitioners, there was no settled course of professional education. As we have seen, ignorant quacks could get away with murder and manslaughter, and lawyers too often held the liberty and lives of clients in their hands. Whatever the cause, however, his dislike was often expressed in his parliamentary speeches and the following are typical examples.

On July 26, 1839, Wakley found before the House of Commons a measure to regulate the appointment of stipendiary magistrates. It required that they be barristers of at least seven years high standing. At that time the period was 10 years. Wakley, however, was not concerned with the term of years at all. Why, he asked, were lawyers of necessity the right persons to inquire into matters of commonsense and justice? "There are," he complained, "no men to be met within society so utterly destitute of commonsense as lawyers." He also strongly objected to the choice being limited to gentlemen of the Bar. One day, he said, they were engaged in showing that truth was falsehood, the next in proving that falsehood was truth; their understanding, therefore, became so perverted that they ever afterwards found the greatest difficulty in separating the one from the other. "The effect of such measures as this," he concluded, "would be to convert the whole Bar into a set of government toadeaters."

When it came to the remuneration of lawyers Wakley explained on April 13, 1840, in a debate on the proposed salary of £14,000 for the Admiralty Judge, that in his view at least, "whatever might be the learning, whatever the ingenuity, and whatever the skill of the man, no lawyer is, or in my opinion ever will be, worth more than £3,000 a year."

Some support for Wakley's general view of the profession may be gleaned from its own journals of the day. The *Law Review,* for example, condemned in strong terms those barristers who it claimed put financial rewards before professional integrity and after referring to some cases involving gross misconduct, went so far as to suggest appointing a watchdog with power to institute proceedings against barristers who acted unprofessionally. Later, the *Law Magazine* attacked what it called "scandalous offendings" at the Bar. Outside the profession the *Examiner* complained that barristers were "advocates of falsehood for a guinea," and that in the very temple of justice "they glory in procuring the triumph of the wrong-doer." Clearly the opinion of Sir S. Sprigge that Wakley's attitude was inexplicable, subjective and unreasonable cannot be sustained.

Wakley also continued to wage war on medical malpractice and quacks, even when to do so involved a conflict with personal friendship. One such case was that of Dr. John Elliotson, for long a friend of Wakley and a frequent contributor to *The Lancet.* It was a bizarre incident. Dr. Elliotson was senior physician to the University College Hospital and Professor of Medicine in the medical school. He was extremely popular with colleagues, students and the public and Thackeray dedicated his novel *Pendennis* to him. In fact in what follows his good faith was never questioned, only his judgment. Ever looking for new methods of treatment he had the misfortune to become interested in experiments in mesmerism carried out by a Baron Dupotet in Paris. The Baron claimed that his methods could relieve, and even cure, epilepsy. Unfortunately Elliotson saw them as a possible cure for much else besides and employed two mediums, Elizabeth and Jane O'Key. Although only 17, Elizabeth was clever and shrewd but Jane was only a pale imitation of her sister. These two girls, when hypnotized, would twist into convulsions on being touched by fluids and metals previously charged with "magnetism" by Elliotson. Worse than that they would answer questions as to the proper treatment of the doctor's patients. So-called animal magnetism, transferred vision and telepathy were used but produced no viable results only mysticism and even a degree of indecency.

Why Elliotson's good faith was never doubted is far from clear. The governors of the hospital were unhappy with the experiments but a majority of the students supported Elliotson who argued that all innovators are held to be mad or dishonest and what is improbable today becomes routine tomorrow. Wakley attacked the experiments in *The Lancet* and queried whether the O'Keys were or were not honest and trustworthy. And if they were imposters was the doctor a dupe or a rogue? Elliotson could not ignore the challenge. He offered to bring his mediums to Wakley and demonstrate their powers to him. Accordingly, on August 16, 1838, experiments were conducted in the drawing room at 35 Bedford Square before a selected audience. Elliotson claimed that Elizabeth O'Key would fall into convulsions when touched by a disc of magnetic nickel but remain unmoved when in contact with a disc of lead. Both metals were handed to Wakley who, unnoticed, gave the nickel disc to J.F. Clarke who, with Baron Dupotet, was present at Elliotson's request. Clarke put the disc in his pocket and moved away.

Wakley then leaned forward and touched the girl's hand with the lead disc. At this point a member of the audience loudly whispered, "take care that you do not apply the nickel too strongly." When the girl immediately fell into convulsions Elliotson declared that no metal but nickel had ever produced such effects. Wakley then explained the trick and declared the girl an imposter. Elliotson persisted and claimed that somehow the power of the nickel had been present so further experiments continued for the remainder of the day and the following day. "Mesmerized" water and "mesmerized" gold were used but the girls began more and more to respond in the wrong way. Without attacking Elliotson Wakley denounced the whole charade in *The Lancet* with a detailed account of the performance. The Council of University College thereupon took the opportunity to ban the use of such methods in the future and Elliotson felt obliged to resign his posts. With sincere regrets about the doctor, the students endorsed the action of the Council by only a small majority.

CHAPTER 6

THE PEOPLE'S JUDGE

We have already seen how important Wakley considered the election of medical men as coroners to be, and that he himself had stood for the office in East Middlesex in 1830. No other opportunity presented itself until nine years later when, in January 1839, the coronership of West Middlesex fell vacant. There were a number of cogent reasons why Wakley should accept the call to stand again. At the time inquests were frequently held in tap rooms and taverns where alcohol was freely available. The Sol's Arms in *Bleak House* gives a grim and potent picture. A typical case was reported in *The Times* for June 6, 1839, when in an inquest on a particularly gruesome body the "courtroom" in "The Rough" public house in Westminster was adjourned in uproar because of the oppressive atmosphere. Wakley was alarmed that many such inquests degenerated into farce either from a surfeit of gin or the incompetence of legal coroners. He had continued to campaign for medical coroners in the columns of *The Lancet* during those nine years and had reported numerous inquests which made clear his reasons.

In one case, for example, a family ate a pie from which two of them died at once, a third some 24 hours later, and a fourth was seriously sick. The remnants of the pie were thrown out into the yard where some chickens ate them and died instantly. All the evidence pointed to arsenic poisoning, yet the coroner directed the jury to bring in a verdict of "death by the visitation of God". Later, when the bodies were exhumed, poisoning by arsenic was established and divine intervention exploded. Wakley always claimed that this travesty of justice could never have occurred with a medical coroner.

In another poisoning case, where prussic acid was used, the

coroner, who did not know the fatal dose of the acid, misdirected the jury who found "suicide during temporary derangement" where there was no evidence at all pointing towards either suicide or insanity. In a case where a woman named Elizabeth Chalk had died from cholera, which was prevalent at the time, the coroner told the jury to return a verdict of manslaughter after refusing to admit the testimony of four medical witnesses but allowing three young children to say she was pushed about. On the other hand when a jury wished to find manslaughter in a case where a 15-year-old youth had died after a vicious assault, and the autopsy had revealed severe damage to the brain, the coroner overruled them. He informed the jury that a verdict of manslaughter would cost the parish £100 to £150 and that the accused would probably be acquitted anyway at his subsequent trial. These are only a small fraction of such cases reported in *The Lancet.* Added to which legal coroners had largely frustrated the purpose of Wakley's *Medical Witnesses Act* by refusing to call medical witnesses on the ground of economy.

It is interesting to note that in her novel *Middlemarch* George Eliot reveals some of the contemporary attitudes to Wakley and the coronership of medical men. She writes:

"I hope," says Mr. Chiceley, "you are not one of *The Lancet's* men, Mr. Lydgate - wanting to take the coronership out of the hands of the legal profession: your words appear to point that way." "I disapprove of Wakley," interposed Dr. Sprague, "no man more: he is an ill-intentioned fellow, who would sacrifice the respectability of the profession, which everybody knows depends on the London Colleges, for the sake of getting some notoriety for himself ..." "But Wakley is right sometimes," the Doctor added, judicially. "I could mention one or two points on which Wakley is in the right."

The group continued to discuss the relative merits of legal against medical coroners with Lydgate adding: "A lawyer is no better than an old woman at a *post-mortem* examination. How is he to know the action of a poison? You might as well say that scanning verse will teach you to scan the potato crops." It is a remarkable tribute to Wakley and his public fame that he should thus appear in a work of fiction by so great an artist.

To return to West Middlesex in 1839, we find Wakley faced with severe financial problems. These resulted from the purchase of a country estate at Harefield Park near Uxbridge, his luxurious style of living in Bedford Square and the need to support his family and educate his children. He was, in consequence, deterred by the prospective expense of an election (it had cost £7,000 in 1830) which might seriously jeopardize the existence of *The Lancet.* However, once again friends came forward to help and he was persuaded to stand as a candidate. He had to face 9,000 freeholders with the vote in an extremely far-flung division stretching as it did from Farringdon Road adjacent to the City in the east to Uxbridge in the west. It comprised over 300 square miles, which was daunting indeed for electioneering.

And there were political obstacles. The Tory Middlesex magistrates, who paid the coroner's fees, were openly hostile to Radical Wakley and decided to intervene. Without warning, on February 7, they petitioned the Lord Chancellor, Lord Cottenham, to withdraw the writ he had issued to commence the election on February 18. They asked him to declare that two coroners should be elected for the one vacancy, each to act for one half of the division. This would at least ensure the election of their own candidate. The bias was only too obvious, however, since they had been satisfied with the previous coroner, a Mr. Stirling, who had not only acted alone, even at the age of 94, but was also a practising solicitor and clerk to the very same magistrates. It was not only *The Lancet* that pointed to the prejudice but also the *Globe,* the *Examiner* and the *Morning Chronicle.* It cannot have escaped the Lord Chancellor, either since he brusquely rejected the request. In consequence, after Wakley had secured 2,015 votes to 582 for his solicitor opponent the latter retired from the contest and on February 25, Wakley found himself elected coroner for West Middlesex. Even at that stage Wakley's enemies were still trying to persuade his opponent to continue the hopeless contest simply to increase his expenses.

Soon after the election Wakley issued new regulations providing that the Coroner should be informed of deaths occurring within his jurisdiction in the following cases:

1. When persons die suddenly.
2. When persons are found dead.
3. When persons die from any acts of violence or any accident.
4. When women die during labour or a few hours after delivery.
5. When persons are supposed to have died from the effects of poisons or quack medicines.
6. When persons die who appear to have been neglected during sickness or extreme poverty.
7. When persons die in confinement, as in prisons, police offices, or station houses.
8. When lunatics or paupers die in confinement, whether in public or in private asylums.

Such a measure was long overdue but this did not prevent indignant uproar and this time the magistrates secured more support by suggesting that Wakley's motive was to increase his fees. Newspapers such as *The Times, The Observer, The Morning Herald* and the *Morning Advertiser* joined the fray and all published leading articles hostile to the regulations on the ground that they would unnecessarily increase the number of inquests. The desirability of the measure for victims of unlawful acts and omissions and their families seems to have escaped the imagination of the editors.

Wakley, ever willing to hit back, responded in a vigorous speech to one of his juries. The coroner, he explained, was the people's Judge, the only Judge the people had the power to appoint. The office had been specially instituted for the protection of the people and the spleen against him came from certain persons in authority who had been, and who wished to continue to be, free from observation and control. To which the *Morning Herald* reported that: "It all tends to the hustings. This villainous iteration about *the people, the people, the people,* has very little to do with the coroner's quest but it has a vast deal to do with the next election for Finsbury." Certain sections of the medical press also "warned" the profession that Wakley was out to "terrorize" them.

To the unprejudiced observer, however, Wakley was soon to be vindicated. On September 30, 1839, just 24 hours after the new regulations had come into force, Thomas Austin, aged 79 and a pauper, died in the Hendon Workhouse. In fact, he had fallen into the copper in the laundry and did not survive the scalding he received. In breach of the new regulations no notice was given to the coroner and with indecent haste the Guardians ordered the body to be buried in the Hendon churchyard without delay. Wakley heard of the death, however, and swiftly attended at the workhouse to hold an inquest. The Guardians resisted, but Wakley demanded that the body be exhumed and the inquest was held. The jury returned a verdict of accidental death, but added a rider that the workhouse authorities were guilty of contributory negligence in not placing a railing around the copper. The Master of the workhouse resented this and endeavoured to embarrass the coroner. After the verdict was given he exclaimed in triumph: "The jury have found a verdict, but have not identified the body." To which Wakley blandly inquired: "If this is not the body of the man who was killed in your vat, pray, Sir, how many paupers have you boiled?"

Notwithstanding, Wakley's enemies joined battle once more. At a meeting of magistrates called at Clerkenwell Sessions House the Rev. Theodore Williams, the vicar of Hendon and a magistrate, formally complained of Wakley's conduct. He suggested Wakley's fees be refused, despite their already having been passed by the finance committee, and that the Lord Chancellor be petitioned to remove him from the coronership. In an attempt to humiliate Wakley and discredit his honesty the meeting appointed a committee to inquire into the increase in inquests and consider the fees which, together with expenses, could only be paid if approved by the magistrates. The *Morning Chronicle* rushed headlong into the attack with the story of an inquest "got up for the sake of securing a fee" under a heading "Mr. Wakley's Coronership." It then had to withdraw even more rapidly when Wakley threatened libel proceedings that could not fail since the paper had overlooked the fact that the case had occurred 10 months before Wakley was elected coroner and when the post was still held by Mr. Stirling.

Other papers continued the harassment, however, until the magistrates' committee published its findings. To wide astonishment, after all the hubbub, the committee found that Wakley was holding less inquests than his predecessor, that less money had been paid for the attendance of medical witnesses and that Wakley's expenses per inquest were considerably lower than those of Mr. Baker, the coroner for East Middlesex. At last, Wakley was able to establish to a listening audience that proper inquiries could often reveal that a death was of natural causes and thus avoid the necessity of an inquest. On the other hand sudden death in the institutions mentioned in his regulations was often caused by cruelty and negligence and these would be exposed by inquest where necessary. For example, shortly after the Austin case Wakley was called upon to inquire into the death from hypothermia in the same Hendon Union of a diabetic who was locked in an unheated room in bitterly cold weather. His "crime" was to have asked for leave to visit his family. Such public investigation before a jury had a salutary effect in improving conditions in workhouses.

The magistrates were not to be denied, however, and were still intent on pursuing Wakley. Matters came to a head when some men suspected of murder were committed to prison at Clerkenwell. Wakley held that they had a right to hear the evidence against them and demanded their presence at the inquest prior to the magistrates' preliminary hearing which would otherwise be their first intimation of the prosecution case. The prison governor refused to produce them. Heatedly, and accurately, Wakley stressed to the inquest jury the antiquity of the coroner's office compared with that of magistrates who had not been heard of before the reign of Edward III with the Justices of the Peace Act, 1361. He then promptly adjourned the inquest saying the coroner must take precedence over the magistrates. To secure his point he sought an interview with the Home Secretary, Lord Normanby, and secured from him a ruling that prisoners should not be committed for trial until they had been before a coroner's jury. The prison governor conceded defeat and the prisoners attended the resumed inquest.

Notwithstanding, the magistrates accused Wakley of usurping their functions by his juries' findings and of holding some inquests by deputy when he was ill. They now wanted a Parliamentary Select Committee to investigate their charges including a further allegation of holding unnecessary inquests as in the case of Thomas Austin. Wakley welcomed the proposal and the Committee was appointed on March 17,

1840, with Wakley as one of its 15 members. It reported at the end of July and completely exonerated Wakley. Yet, with two years of bitter attacks, the magistrates had succeeded in doing some damage to Wakley's reputation. For that he never forgave them although from this time on a truce existed between them. Wakley continued to hold an average of 15 inquests a week and where medical evidence was important the cases were published in *The Lancet* in order to enlighten the public and justify medical coroners.

On Saturday, June 10, 1843 Wakley was appointed chairman of a Committee of Coroners at a meeting held in the Salopian Coffee House, Charing Cross Road. Two days later he was writing to Sir Robert Peel thanking him, on behalf of the Committee, for receiving a deputation and discussing their problem in an "extremely urbane and polite manner". What they wanted was a fair and adequate remuneration for their services. Apparently their fees had been fixed at 20 shillings for each inquest, with an allowance of ninepence a mile for travelling expenses, by a Statute of George II in 1752. Not only had there been no subsequent increase but in 1818 the Court of King's Bench, in a freak ruling in *R.* v. *Justices of Oxfordshire,* had reduced the travelling expenses by providing that they should be paid for the outward journey only. Now the coroners wanted a fee of 30 shillings and one shilling and sixpence per mile both to and from the inquest, although later Wakley was to help secure salaries for coroners in place of fees and thereby destroy any possible pecuniary temptation to hold unnecessary inquests.

Death by Flogging

A punishment which particularly roused Wakley to anger was whipping. In a time when many punishments were harsh, whipping was accepted by public opinion as suitable for petty offenders. These included vagrants, persons convicted of small thefts, parents of illegitimate children, political offenders, and unsuccessful prosecutors who could not pay costs. It was often carried out with the offender tied to a moving cart in a public street as is still attested today by the narrow street in the City of York named "Whip-ma-Whop-ma-Gate", after the practice operated there, a short distance from the city gaol. Up to 50 lashes appears to have been the usual sentence and it sometimes caused dumbness, mental deterioration, permanent injury, or even death.

Floggings in the army and navy, as well as in the prison service, were also a regular occurrence and could involve up to 200 lashes with a cat-o'-nine tails, a thong made even more lethal by a number of knots. Pertinently, the *Law Magazine* was later to comment that, "while the lash is used in the army and navy, no one can logically object to it for felons."

It was on February 25, 1836 that Wakley had first moved in the House of Commons, in a debate on the Mutiny Bill, that flogging in the army should be abolished. He knew that if he succeeded in this the other services would follow. He had seen, he told the House, the body of William Saundry who had died from a flogging at Woolwich Barracks. He had been sentenced to 200 lashes with the cat which had nine thongs treated until they resembled wire. In the course of the "punishment" his screams were so loud that the fifes and drums were ordered to drown them. Yet still they could be heard 1½ miles away. After 100 lashes, or as Wakley pointed out, 900 thongs, had been passed over his lacerated back he had to be taken down. The Member for Dumfries, continued Wakley, had said flogging was not degrading to the soldier. If it was not degrading to the men, asked Wakley wryly, why was it not applied to the officers?

Despite the passion and the justice of his pleading Wakley was not successful on that occasion. However, 10 years later he had another opportunity and this time he was in a position to take action himself. On June 15, 1846, Frederick John White, a private of the Seventh Hussars, received a severe and cruel flogging of 150 lashes with the cat-o'-nine tails at the Cavalry Barracks on Hounslow Heath after an enforced 17 hours fast. Several soldiers who witnessed the flogging fainted on the spot. White was even refused a drink of tea whilst in agony after the flogging. Unfortunately for the government the death was within Wakley's jurisdiction as coroner. White died on July 11, 1846 and fortunately for the truth the local vicar was sceptical of the reported death from illness. He finally elicited that the flogging had occurred, whereupon he refused permission for the funeral and informed the coroner. Wakley promptly attended the scene and summoned a jury to hold an inquest. Without really examining White's back three army doctors declared that the death had nothing to do with the flogging and, following a question from Dr. John Bowring, Bentham's executor and MP for Bolton, this was repeated in the House of Commons by Fox Maule on behalf of the government on July 20.

A local surgeon who examined the body at Wakley's request also suspiciously failed to examine the back and the spine and Wakley rejected his report. He then called in a specialist, Erasmus Wilson of the Middlesex Hospital, who, after examining the lacerated body, had no difficulty in convincing the jury that the flogging had caused the death. In giving their verdict the jury, who had also seen White's body, took their cue from Wakley and publicly expressed their "horror and disgust" at the law which permitted the "revolting punishment of flogging to be inflicted upon British soldiers". They implored every man in the Kingdom to join "hand and heart" in forwarding petitions to the legislature praying for the abolition of such a disgraceful practice, which was a "slur upon the humanity and fair name of the people of this country."

Serious public concern was instantly aroused, and on August

7, Lord John Russell announced in the Commons that the Duke of Wellington, as Commander in Chief, had given directions to army officers that the maximum number of lashes should be reduced from 200 to 50. Introducing a Motion to endorse this, Russell explained that he desired to keep the army in a high state of discipline without corporal punishment, but thought the Duke right to retain a maximum of 50 lashes.

Bowring immediately moved an Amendment to abolish flogging in the army altogether. "Necessity," he said, "had always been used as a justification by tyrants, even for the slave trade and 1,500 lashes." Wakley, in the debate, pointed out that 50 lashes could be worse than 200 according to the length and weight of the cat, the type of thong used, whether it had six or 12 knots, and how long the flogging took. He defended his action in calling the inquest with great skill, but in view of his involvement wisely left the main burden of the assault on flogging as a punishment to Bowring.

At some length Bowring quoted soul-sickening accounts of floggings in the army. These included reports of Dr. Ferguson, Inspector General of Military Hospitals, who claimed to have attended, and stopped, numerous floggings, and a Dr. Marshall who in *Military Miscellany* had written, "for eight years it was my disgusting duty to flog men at least three times a week." In appalling detail these doctors described the acts of flogging and their toll in reducing strong, tough men to the state of babbling imbeciles, often for nothing more than trivial offences of discipline. Bowring also recalled that Bentham had been "tortured" in consequence of his residence being adjacent to a flogging-yard, and had often spoken of his agony when he heard the shrieks of soldiers under the lash.

Among the worst features of flogging, Bowring continued in Benthamite vein, was that as a punishment it was uncertain. It had to depend on the strength, dexterity and animus of the flogger, the length of the handle, the character of the cord, and the number and size of the knots, none of which was regulated by law. And he did not omit to include the susceptibility of the sufferer. In the event Bowring's amendment was defeated, but as a result of Wakley's swift action, coupled with his fine eloquence and fierce anger on hearing of the death of White, he roused the whole nation and flogging in the army largely fell into disuse until it was finally abolished by the Army Act of 1881. Nevertheless Wakley was attacked for partiality. As usual he counter-attacked. First, by producing a tribute from Mr. Trimmer, the vicar of Heston, to whom the case had been reported as death from liver complaint when request was made for burial of White. Then, another from the solicitor who had held a watching brief for the officers of the Seventh Hussars. And finally, from a barrister and retired Indian Judge who had also been present at the inquest.

However, in the general public acclaim that Wakley had achieved, inevitably one sour note was struck. Although Wakley encouraged medical articles in *The Lancet* arguing for and against the verdict of death by flogging, the *Medical Times,* which had been started in opposition to *The Lancet* in 1839, accused Wakley of being advocate instead of Judge and of having taken refuge in a "hireling witness and a hugger-mugger autopsy." He had made a farcical impersonation of a Judge who "suggests, insinuates, applauds, encourages, assails, twists, twirls and manoeuvres in every shape, form and direction to conjure up against an honest practitioner a fictitious semblance of murder!" And, again the imputation, all because he wanted a public sensation to help his fortunes in a forthcoming election.

Some of these outrageous allegations appeared even while the jury were still sitting. Not surprisingly, Wakley moved for a criminal information (equivalent to an accusation of felony) in the Queen's Bench. But he was unsuccessful on the peculiar ground that on an earlier occasion when Wakley had defended himself against another libel by the editor of the paper, a man named Healey, he had replied in like manner. Healey had a profound hatred of Wakley and constantly used the columns of the *Medical Times* to render suspect his morality and honesty. Wakley generally ignored the libels stating that he did not believe such a trashy paper was read by the profession and that Healey's motives and stupidity were so obvious that if he were allowed enough rope he was sure to cheat the executioner at the Old Bailey.

On the prompting of his constituents, however, Wakley did issue civil proceedings in February 1847 at the conclusion of which the proprietors of the paper, including Healey, were ordered to pay £150 damages with costs and were severely criticized by the Judge. The printers of the paper thereupon apologized to Wakley and declined further publication. Healey, however, attacked the integrity of the Judge, Chief Baron Pollock, and made it his aim in life to destroy Wakley. Further successful proceedings followed but Wakley failed to obtain his criminal information.

On this occasion the Middlesex magistrates supported Wakley. Even so attacks on him continued, both inside and outside the House of Commons, until his virtues as coroner were finally apparent to all. In the meantime, nothing was allowed to deter him from inveighing against medical malpractices and he was particularly concerned to protect children - though not always successfully. In one case in 1848 a girl of 14 had been tied to a bedpost by her mother and the room locked while the mother went out for the day. On the mother's return the girl was found dead having been strangled whilst attempting to sit down. Wakley placed the mother in custody, heard the evidence and committed her for manslaughter. At her trial the jury found her guilty but the Judge thought there was no premeditated cruelty and sentenced her to one year only. It might not have been surprising if Wakley had suggested that Judges too should have medical knowledge and experience.

In another case the issue was whether the mother of a dead baby had committed murder or merely concealment of birth. A beadle was ordered to summon a jury and how Charles Dickens became a member of it has been described by the author himself:

> The beadle did what melancholy did to the youth in Gray's Elegy - he marked me for his own. And the way in which the beadle did it was this: he summoned me as a juryman on coroner's inquests. In my feverish alarm I repaired "for safety and for succour" - like those sagacious Northern shepherds who, having had no previous reason whatever to believe in young Norval, very prudently did not originate the hazardous idea of believing in him - to a deep householder. This profound man informed me that the beadle counted on my buying him off, on my bribing him not to summon me, and that if I would attend an inquest with a cheerful countenance and profess alacrity in that branch of my country's service the beadle would be disheartened and would give up the game. I roused my energies, and the next time the wily beadle summoned me I went. The beadle was the blankest beadle I ever looked on when I answered to my name, and his discomfiture gave me courage to go through with it.

It is interesting to note that one of Wakley's later reforms was to replace the beadle by a coroner's officer. This inquest was held in 1841 in the parish workhouse and Dickens confessed his unsuitability as a juror by having a considerable prejudice in favour of the more humane verdict. Apparently the mother, a young girl, had given birth to the child and immediately afterwards had been obliged to clean her mistress's doorstep. Dickens notes the lack of sympathy towards the weak and ill girl before them, the brutality of the mistress and the solitary misery of the orphan girl. He decided to cross-examine the mistress:

> I took heart to ask this witness a question or two which hopefully admitted of an answer which might give a favourable turn to the case. She made the turn as little favourable as it could be, but it did some good, and the coroner, who was nobly patient and humane (he was the late Mr. Wakley), cast a look of strong encouragement in my direction ... I tried again and the coroner backed me again, for which I ever afterwards felt grateful to him, as I do now to his memory, and we got another favourable turn out of some other witness, some member of the family with a strong prepossession against the sinner. I think we had the doctor back again, and I know that the coroner summed up for our side and that I and my British brothers turned round to discuss our verdict and get ourselves into great difficulties with our large chairs and the broker. At that stage of the case I tried hard again, being convinced that I had cause for it, and at last we found for the offence of only concealing the birth.

It is a fitting commentary on Wakley from a man who was himself a notable scourge to officialdom and officials. The verdict of the jury was concealment of birth and when the girl was in prison awaiting trial Dickens made sure she had some comforts and paid for counsel to represent her at the trial where she was treated leniently. "I regard this" concludes Dickens, "as a very notable uncommercial experience, because this good came of a beadle. And to the best of my knowledge, information and belief it is the only good that ever did come of a beadle since the first beadle put on his cocked hat."

Many of Wakley's inquests raised points of medical and legal interest. His view on the workings of the Poor Law, on the proper interpretation of the physical signs of death, on poisonous doses of dangerous drugs and the need for emergency treatment all helped to raise his reputation as a great coroner. At a time when babies could be sold to "minders" for £4 each and promptly murdered it is well to remember Wakley's critical role in securing proper medical witnesses which led to the formidable expert forensic witness of today in cases of sudden death.

Rout of the Bashaws of Somerset House

As already indicated Wakley inevitably became deeply involved with the Poor Law. Prior to 1834 the Poor Law was still based on the famous Act of Elizabeth I in 1601 which made every one of the 15,000 parishes in the land responsible for supporting its poor. This became open to abuse in the nineteenth century when the new manufacturers in the towns could take men from the villages when work was plentiful and return them there for outdoor relief when it was scarce. Nevertheless, under the Speenhamland system, introduced on May 6, 1797, low wages were subsidized out of the local rates to a figure based upon the size of families and the price of bread. This system introduced by Berkshire magistrates and known as the "bread and children" scale was never law but was almost universally adopted in the Midlands and southern England. For the next 40 years the system kept the poor at subsistence level but not destitute. Unfortunately, over the years the system swelled with corruption and abuse. And naturally it encouraged employers to keep wages low. Not surprisingly the cost of administering the Poor Law rose from £619,000 in 1750 to £8,000,000 in 1818.

Then in 1830 serious agrarian disturbances erupted when labourers began to claim their allowances as of right. The Whigs decided something must be done and in 1832 they appointed a Commission of Inquiry in line with the general Benthamite fervour for root-and-branch reform that was sweeping the country. All the same this crucial commission failed to inquire into the causes of poverty and its reports were stigmatized for relying on partial statistics. It proposed that outdoor relief be abolished for the able-bodied and that relief be given in "well-regulated" workhouses based on the principle of "less eligibility". This meant that conditions in them had to be worse than any outside and they were often derisively called "gaols without guilt". Even Edwin Chadwick, whose enthusiasm knew no bounds, was unwittingly to describe them as uninviting places of wholesome restraint.

Worse still, to compound the horror men, women and children were to be mercilessly kept apart. The previously independent parishes were to be grouped into unions with a strong central authority - the Poor Law Commission - to enforce a uniform policy. Even so there was to be no national system of relief, so inequality was unavoidable. Pursuant to a pitiless philosophy poverty was presented as a crime which invoked deep disgrace. Its chief purpose was to drive workers on to the labour market by the abolition of outdoor relief. These proposals became law with the enactment of the Poor Law Amendment Act of 1834 in the face of opposition from the great majority of newspapers and public opinion. Before long the strong feeling against the new "Bastilles" and the "three Bashaws of Somerset House" helped give rise to Chartism.

Wakley, with his true sensitivity to the sufferings of the poor, attacked the Act with contempt and passion at every opportunity. He depicted the workhouse as a cruel prison, the rich as persecuting the poor, and the central authority as a pack of lazy, underworked, overfed officials paid from the public purse. A rule of silence was enforced at all meals which provoked Wakley to point out that the silent system was generally regarded as the most severe form of punishment in prison life. As for central control, when the Dewsbury Guardians wished to allow an old man to smoke a pipe they first had to obtain the leave of the Commissioners. And when, at Wakley's instigation, a Parliamentary Committee was formed to investigate the scandal of Andover's workhouse in 1846 it was found that inmates were so starved that they fought among themselves for gristle and marrow in putrid bones they were given the task of crushing.

According to Mr. Etwall, the MP for Andover, the decomposing bones were two to three months old. Yet when a bone was turned out of the heap the inmates scrambled for it like a pack of dogs and the man who got it was obliged to run away and hide before he could eat the marrow. The Master of the Workhouse, he said, had caused this by defrauding the inmates of their food and had meted out particularly harsh and cruel treatment to children. One employee had foolishly mentioned what he had seen and was instantly dismissed.

The parliamentary inquiry was fully reported in *The Times*, but it is a startling exposure of Victorian values to read in Hansard the reply to Etwall given by Sir James Graham, Peel's Home Secretary in 1846. According to Graham it was melancholy that so much precious time of the House should have been consumed in a matter which after all was only a workhouse squabble. He was, however, opposed to this method of employment (bone crushing) which had now been suppressed, against the wishes of nearly 100 Unions.

Enraged at what had been revealed Wakley took the opportunity to attack the "vast and extraordinary" powers of the Commissioners which, although unconstitutional, had been exercised without question or interference for 10 years. What had been revealed could not with any propriety be termed "a workhouse squabble". It was an atrocious evil. A wider inquiry into the Commissioners and their cover-up of the investigation was called for and Wakley and his supporters won a tremendous victory when the Commissioners were subsequently removed from office.[1]

To Wakley the Act was vicious, irrelevant, absurd and malevolent. And the medical problems it caused did not escape his pen. There was excessive mortality in the workhouses. Basing himself on official returns, he wrote in 1841, "... out of 12,313 poor people in workhouses 2,552 perished in one year!" A much higher proportion than out of doors where, for example, only 382 out of a similar number had died in the insanitary slum district of St. Giles in London. Wakley took into account the fact that there was a greater proportion of old people in the workhouses. Also that some were taken in sick. But he used statistics, including those of the Poor Law Commissioners' own reports, to show that these considerations made little serious difference and to conclude that, "the diseases which prove so fatal, therefore, assail the poor after their entrance into these *ante-chambers of the grave.*"

Wakley spoke in the House of Commons on a number of occasions on the causes of excessive mortality, on the treatment of insane paupers and on the low pay of poor-law medical officers. More than once he launched an onslaught against the terrible sufferings of the fettered and molested prisoners in private asylums for the insane and he managed to secure important reforms. But cruelty to lunatics was not confined to private asylums. After his death two serious tragedies occurred in workhouses in 1864 and 1865 which roused public opinion to such an extent that his son James, wearing his father's mantle, was able to institute a wide-ranging inquiry and publish its report in *The Lancet.*

1.   A useful corrective to many newspaper exaggerations of the horrors of the Poor Law is to be found in David Roberts "How Cruel was the Victorian Poor Law?" *Historical Journal* 6 (1963): 97-107. Nevertheless Wakley's revulsion and his changes were fully justified as both the parliamentary inquiry and the dismissal of the Commissioners proved.

One of the tragedies occurred at Flushing in Cornwall where a man incarcerated for 20 years was found by a visitor "naked and buried in ordure". His bed proved to be a flagstone covered with human excreta to a depth of four inches in which the mark of his body was clearly visible. The *Lancet* report of the case was headed: "The Horrible Story" and the question arose whether this was a normal state of affairs bearing in mind that there were some 40,000 inmates of asylums of one kind or another. To resolve the doubt James instituted "The Lancet Sanitary Commission for Investigating into the state of Workhouse Infirmaries."

The Commission produced detailed reports on individual infirmaries and they were all published in *The Lancet* and thence, in summary, into the general press. Some infirmaries, such as that in Islington which lay within Thomas Wakley's former jurisdiction, received a clean bill of health. Others were more grim. Often the ordinary sick were jumbled in with imbeciles and lunatics in frightful conditions which caused many deaths from diseases. In fact a large number of infirmaries were found to be fit for nothing but to be destroyed and as a consequence of *The Lancet* reports many were condemned and a number of new and improved workhouse hospitals were built.

The Ballot.

LONDON, SUNDAY JANUARY 2, 1831.

The APPEAL of the ELECTORS of PRESTON to the PEOPLE of ENGLAND, SCOTLAND, and IRELAND.—Unanimously agreed to at a Public Meeting, held this day.

Fellow Countrymen and Brothers,

"THE time is come" when we want your aid ; we crave your powerful co-operation; we call upon you to assist us to secure the fruit of that victory, which we have attained by an unexampled struggle, during the last eight days. The blow is struck ! 3730 brave, honest, and patriotic men, who live by the toil of their hands and the sweat of their brows. Electors of this Borough, have by their unbought votes, chosen HENRY HUNT. Esq., as their Representative ; we know him as the long-tried friend and fearless advocate of the just rights of the People, and we believe him to be the very best man in the kingdom, to convey, within the walls of Parliament, the sentiments, the wishes, and the wants of all those, who, like ourselves, live upon, and who are anxious to live upon, the honest fruits of their labour.

Mr. Stanley has demanded a Scrutiny !!!—Men of England, there is not the slightest pretence for this. There never was a fairer Election on the part of the people than this. Mr. Stanley knows that we are poor ; he has felt that we are honest; he knows that we have made unexampled sacrifices—and that we have endured even the most heart-rending privations during this glorious struggle for free-dom; and therefore it was, when he fled from Preston last night, that he with a satanic smile urged his myrmidons of the law, to harass, to oppress, and to weary us out by procrastination, and by every species of low cunning and fraud, to hem us down with such heavy expenses, as, he believes, we are not able to sustain. Coun-trymen and Brothers, will you stand silently by with your arms folded, and not lend a hand to save the country from this everlasting disgrace?

We ask not your assistance, or participation in any violent mea-sures, to which we are as much averse as you can be ; we know too well whom we have to deal with, and are determined strictly to act upon Mr. Hunt's advice to avoid committing any breach of the peace, which, we are sure with him, is the last, forlorn hope of Mr. Stanley. But as we are men who have nothing but what we work hard for, we do earnestly and confidently appeal to you as Brothers, to give us—and give us promptly too—your pecuniary assistance. Nelson said before going into battle, "England expect's every man to do his duty." This exclamation will apply with treble force on the present occa-sion. A Scrutiny indeed ! "List, oh list!" Countrymen and Bro-thers ; a scrutiny is called for by Mr. Stanley, and why you shall hear. There were ten poll clerks employed, nine out of the ten voted for Mr. Stanley, contrary to every principle of justice, or even of common decency ; Mr. Stanley had ten check clerks, and twenty inspectors, all paid and all voted; and he had nine-tenths of the at-torneys in Preston, and every-body knows that an attorney never works without being paid—they, nearly 50 in number, all voted for Mr. Stanley; he had the parish officers with their books ready to send back any pauper who came to poll for us, and there never was a body of electors, under any circumstances, that had to encounter so strict and so vigilant a scrutiny as those electors had who tendered their votes for Mr. Hunt. In addition to these, all the public-houses were open, and treating, drinking, and bribery, were as unblushingly and as openly practised as at the late contest for the Borough of Evesham, or any rotten Borough in existence ; while, on the other hand, we were all volunteers—not one man was paid amongst us, not one man can-vassed—but with the honest hearts and votes of the electors, backed up by the enthusiastic support of the women of Preston, we accom-plished, even before Mr. Hunt's arrival amongst us, one of the most arduous undertakings, and one of the most signal victories ever ob-tained over one of the haughtiest of the haughty Aristocratical fami-lies in the kingdom ; a family which has made the populous town of Preston a rotten Borough for the last 50 years. We have, by one mighty effort, rescued ourselves from the grasp of this haughty fa-mily, and restored the Borough to its native purity. We have thus begun that real Reform in Parliament ourselves, which has been so long prayed for by the People, and which has at length been promised them by the Ministers. We have thought it better to rely upon our own exertions, than trust to the promises of Kings or Princes, or of Ministers. or Parliaments.

May you, Countrymen and Brothers, by your liberal aid, promptly administered, encourage others to follow our example, is the earnest prayer of the gallant men of Preston.

To aid and assist us in defending our just rights, we call on you, fellow Countrymen and Brothers, with the full conviction that this

THE LANCET.

Vol. I.—No. 1.]   LONDON, SUNDAY, October 5, 1823.   [*Price 6d.*

PREFACE.

It has long been a subject of surprise and regret, that in this extensive and intelligent community there has not hitherto existed a work that would convey to the Public, and to distant Practitioners as well as to Students in Medicine and Surgery, reports of the Metropolitan Hospital Lectures.

Having for a considerable time past observed the great and increasing inquiries for such information, in a department of science so pre-eminently useful, we have been induced to offer to public notice a work calculated, as we conceive, to supply in the most ample manner, whatever is valuable in these important branches of knowledge ;—and as the Lectures of Sir Astley Cooper, on the theory and practice of Surgery, are probably the best of the kind delivered in Europe, we have commenced our undertaking with the introductory Address of that distinguished professor, given in the theatre of St. Thomas's Hospital on Wednesday evening last. The Course will be rendered complete in subsequent Numbers.

In addition to Lectures, we purpose giving under the head, Medical and Surgical Intelligence, a correct description of all the important Cases that may occur, whether in England or on any part of the civilized Continent.

Although it is not intended to give graphic representations with each Number, yet, we have made such arrangements with the most experienced surgical draughtsmen, as will enable us occasionally to do so, and in a manner, we trust, calculated to give universal satisfaction.

The great advantages derivable from information of this description, will, we hope, be sufficiently obvious to every one in the least degree conversant with medical knowledge ; any arguments, therefore, to prove

Printed and Published by A. Mead, 201, Strand, opposite St. Clement's Church.

Allhallows Museum (formerly Allhallows Grammar School), Honiton, Devon

IN MEMORY
OF
THOMAS WAKLEY
SURGEON AND CORONER
MEDICAL AND SOCIAL
REFORMER
MEMBER OF PARLIAMENT
FOUNDER AND FIRST
EDITOR OF
THE LANCET
BORN AT LAND FARM
MEMBURY DEVON 1795
DIED IN MADEIRA 1862

Tablet in the Church of St. John Baptist, Membury, Devon

CHAPTER 7

"OF CABBAGES AND KINGS"

In one year alone, with 69 important questions before the House of Commons, Wakley had voted on 51 of them. No other MP came close, with Peel voting on 20, O'Connell on 33 and Hume on 35. During his remaining years in Parliament Wakley was to continue to address himself to an equally formidable variety of topics.

In 1841 Lord Melbourne's government came to an end with a vote of no confidence. In the ensuing General Election Wakley was again returned for Finsbury - this time unopposed. Government, however, passed to the Tories led by Sir Robert Peel. In the new House of Commons Wakley attended as regularly as before, and served on important committees, but he did not speak quite so often. In part this was because the Whigs now attacked the Tory administration and the Radicals were not as isolated as they had been when the Tories were in opposition. Nevertheless, he spoke in favour of the secret ballot, against granting pensions to Lord Chancellors, on many occasions against the methods of the Poor Law Commissioners, against the appointment of lawyers as Lunacy Commissioners and on one occasion against unpaid provincial magistrates whom he described as incompetent oafs. He also castigated the government for reckless expenditure on plumbing at Buckingham Palace in contrast with their parsimony in the treatment of prisoners and paupers.

Despite, or more likely because of, his vigorous style Wakley was usually listened to with respect, but in a speech of April 6, 1842 on Lord Mahon's Copyright Bill he made himself somewhat unpopular. Lord Mahon wanted to extend copyright from 28 to 42 years and as long as the author should live thereafter. He was supported on behalf of authors by Macaulay, once described by Sydney Smith as a "book in breaches". Wakley thought the extension, whilst doing little for authors, would harm publishers and printers. It was an arguable point of view. But, characteristically, he chose to ridicule the claims of authors. And in doing so he recited what he described as Wordsworth's most "namby-pamby" poems, "I met Louisa in the Shade" and "Address to a Butterfly". He then continued, "Give a poet an evening sky, dew, withering leaves and a rivulet and he would make a very respectable poem always." To the derisory laughter this gave rise, he replied, "Why, anybody might do it!" only to be greeted with cries of "try it". He had, he rejoined, adding, "I myself could string such compositions together by the bushel. I could write them by the mile." He was not with Bentham likening poetry to pinpush, however, since he went on to compare authors with scientists whose work was unprotected and accrued to the public good. Milton, Bacon and Shakespeare, he claimed, had made their greatest efforts more for honour than gain.

Wakley's outburst owed much to his own earlier struggles to secure the right to publish surgical lectures in *The Lancet.* Nonetheless, the issue was not the same and he was severely criticized for ridiculing Wordsworth and obstructing the claims of authors. *Punch,* which had been founded only the year before and was then far more bitingly satirical than today, quickly entered the fray. In fact it had already pilloried Wakley as a cynical self-seeker of office. In this, if true, he had proved singularly ineffective. There is, however, no evidence that Wakley was ever other than completely true to his chosen role of fearless radical in permanent opposition to Whig and Tory alike when principle required. But on this occasion he had lain himself open to ridicule and *Punch* seized its opportunity.

It proceeded to publish a poem supposedly submitted by Wakley, whom it depicted as the "Apollo of Parliament", and described it as the greatest work of fiction on record. Warming to its theme the following week, under the heading: "Wakley's Warbler, being Finsbury Fragments by a Coroner," it published no less than three poems entitled, "Lines to a Patient", "Aramantha" and "An Impromptu". The last was said to be by a Mr. Maecenas Pitt, described as a well-known proprietor of the Toy and Marble Warehouse in Seven Dials, and "written on the back of a Petition in the House of Commons."

The joke seems to have been popular for the issue of two weeks later saw a cartoon depicting Wakley wearing a Roman toga with a crown of laurels on his head, clutching a harp and standing on clouds held aloft by two angels. Wakley, it reported, was "booked to be poet laureate as soon as Southey departs." Beneath a heading: "Medical Poetry. Mr. Wakley, the Modern Orpheus", it then published yet another poem. This contained the following lines:

To My Love.

The sun upgetting, The dews at setting,
The leafy treeses, The murmuring breezes,
The kisses glowing, The glances knowing,
The girls all crying, The men all lying;
They move the heart so That I can't part so;
And ere I know it I shine a poet.
O Amaryllis, Or Rose or Phillis,
Or as it may be My Poll or Phoebe,
Don't be so cruel, My darling jewel,
Come on not slackly, * * * * *
- Madam, your servant to command,
J. WAKLEY.

After *Punch* had had its fun matters returned to normal when the House debated the enclosure of common lands. Wakley pressed for the right to inquire into the rightful ownership of land being enclosed by landlords which had been dedicated to the public by custom in former centuries. This was a live issue to Wakley who received assistance from his father's vast store of knowledge accumulated as a Commissioner for the Enclosure of Waste Lands. Henry Wakley was still alive, aged 92, but was to die on August 26 in the same year. Later, in 1844 Wakley supported Duncombe in protesting strongly at the opening by the Foreign Office of letters of the Italian patriot, Joseph Mazzini. The contents of the letters were said to have been passed on to the Austrian authorities and to have led to the death of some of Mazzini's friends abroad.

He also felt keenly about the injustice of the notorious game laws and in 1845 supported a Motion by John Bright, of Anti-Corn Law fame, for the appointment of a Commission of Inquiry into their working. He presented a number of petitions on the subject but again ran into difficulties as he was a skilled sportsman and had a fine sporting estate at Harefield Park - now the site of Harefield Hospital. One Lord pointed to this inconsistency in assisting Bright when he had himself to support the rigid enforcement of the same laws on his own grounds. Wakley freely admitted that he would not allow his pheasants to be stolen but said he would always feed a hungry man and around Harefield a would-be poacher preferred to go to the house and ask for food rather than commit a felony. That was, of course, an exaggeration but, although he did not say so, it was well known in the countryside around Harefield that if Wakley prosecuted a poacher he always supported the man's wife and family while he was in gaol. A position that would have been considered less hypocritical then, than today. In any event, the fact remains that he worked extremely hard to undermine those very laws.

Another attack was launched on the trade unions when, in 1844, a Bill was introduced to consolidate the law relating to them. As with so much consolidating legislation a number of new and controversial measures were slipped into this Bill. One was to enable a single J.P. to issue a warrant for the arrest of any workman said by his employer to be misbehaving whilst at work. The sentence the same J.P. could then inflict on the unfortunate man was up to two months in prison. It is difficult to believe such a provision could be seriously contemplated. Yet it had the support of the Home Secretary, Sir James Graham, as well as Gladstone and only spirited opposition by Wakley, Duncombe and Hume, helped by a group of Disraeli's "Young Englanders" prevented it from disgracing the statute book.

Also in 1844 the House of Commons was the scene of a debate on the Poor Law Amendment Act in which rural arson came under discussion. Wakley considered such crimes were usually committed in parts of the country where educational standards were low and where squiredom was supreme. Mr. Edmond Wodehouse, a Member for Norfolk, protested at this attack on landlords and stated that Wakley himself could tell the House a good deal more about incendiarism. Wakley was immediately on his feet. He had never, he said, made personal remarks about any Member, although he had not always been extended the same courtesy. He required an explanation of the present reference in the presence of the House. It was horrible to suppose the Member had intended what he said. He dare not enter the House again if he did not ask for an investigation of the truth of the remark which was the foulest calumny.

Wakley then proceeded to outline the facts of the case when his home was destroyed by fire and its determination in his favour. Wodehouse smoothly replied that he was glad to have given Wakley an opportunity to explain a matter which had *already remained too long in doubt.* He would tender an apology but Wakley was too lavish in accusing landlords of selfishness. The House was nonplussed and the Speaker adjourned the sitting to the following Monday (this was a Saturday). When the House resumed, Wodehouse made an adequate and unqualified apology and the Prime Minister, Sir Robert Peel, observed that Wakley was an honourable and innocent man who had now received complete reparation for his injured feelings. Wakley expressed his thanks to Wodehouse and the House, and Peel, sensitive to the harm done, sent a long and eloquent letter to Wakley's eldest son, then aged 23, testifying to the complete esteem in which Wakley was held by the entire House. He praised Wakley as a reformer, orator and fine parliamentarian in a remarkable tribute from a great statesman and political antagonist.

Mysterious Deodands

Another legal "punishment" to which Wakley turned his attention was the question of deodands. No one so far has succeeded in tracing the origin in time of the curious punishment of deodands, by which moveable objects which caused death were forfeit. However, they existed as long ago as Anglo-Saxon times and something similar is described by ancient Greek writers. F.W. Maitland, the eminent legal historian, discovered that in early times they were not intended to provide compensation but were objects upon which vengeance might be wreaked before the dead man could lie in peace. By Sir Matthew Hale's time, in the seventeenth century, they were held forfeit to the King, whose almoner distributed their value for charitable purposes including compensating the victims' families. Swords, horses, and carts were obvious targets and although Hale referred to "moveable things" he included a hayrick from which a man fell to his death. Hale also made an economic distinction so that whereas an entire cart would be forfeit if its wheel caused death, with a mill it would be only the wheel; and with earth in a mine which fell and killed a miner only the earth would be deodand, not the whole mine. Serjeant Hawkins, another early jurist, later accepted those exceptions but drew out the general rule that when an object which caused death was in motion at the time not only the offending part, but all things that moved with it were forfeit.

Although deodands were thought to have become obsolete in the eighteenth century, the Benthamite Criminal Law Commissioners, in their Fourth Report in 1839, claimed that the ancient rules for applying such forfeitures still existed but had become unjust, since they were imposed on persons not at fault and in an arbitrary and capricious manner.

This seems to support the evidence of Harry Smith, in a significant article in the *American Journal of Legal History* in 1967, that these "hallowed mysteries", as he calls them, enjoyed a revival in the early nineteenth century as a means of providing compensation for accidents caused by the new factory machines and death-dealing railway engines. Soon after Hale's time the courts had decided against Hawkins that only the offending wheel of a cart which caused death could be forfeit. However, by the nineteenth century there had been another reversal and Smith quotes cases of a railway carriage and a coach and horses being taken as deodands. This was done to ensure the payment of more substantial compensation by the new capitalists, and as, in some instances, the value of the deodand was awarded to the widow or other relatives of the deceased by the Coroner, there was often no delay in payment.

In fact, the Industrial Revolution had given a fresh meaning to deodands and Wakley, who saw their significance and potential in his office of Coroner, ran a campaign to extend them for occupational accidents.

The toll of human life taken by the railways, factories and mills at this time was appalling. But as a consequence of the harsh ruling of *Baker* v. *Bolton* in 1808 there was no right of action for economic loss or solatium on the death of a breadwinner. In the notorious words of Lord Ellenborough: "In a civil court the death of a human being cannot be complained of as an injury." The only hope of compensation was the deodand although juries commonly awarded small sums.

Partly as a consequence of Wakley's efforts to shake up juries, the values attributed to deodands rose rapidly and in 1840 sums of £500 and £600 were given. Then, in 1841, in a case against the newly opened London and Birmingham Railway Company a sum of £2,000 was awarded. This last case proved to be a turning point, however, as in the same year the Queen's Bench held in the Sonning Railway Carriage case that deodands could be awarded only in respect of wilfully committed crimes. Wakley complained that the court had thrown out the £2,000 verdict after the highest legal opinion in the land had said it was justified. Nevertheless, the Queen's Bench Judges disliked workers receiving compensation for injuries and continued to reject other similar cases.

This led, in turn, to the compromise of 1846 when Lord Campbell's Fatal Accidents Act was passed to help the dependants of men killed in accidents through the act or default of another. Campbell, in fact, introduced a Bill for the Abolition of Deodands and his Deaths by Accident Compensation Bill simultaneously and they continued to travel together throughout their passage through Parliament. Clearly the second, which provided very limited financial compensation, was intended to ensure the enactment of the first. Nevertheless, Campbell complained, on the Lords' second reading of the Bills, that he had heard that 80 members of the Commons could be mustered by one railway company alone to vote against them. Presumably they wanted no compensation at all to be payable. On the other hand, they may have been mere figments of Campbell's imagination since his colleagues in effect told him not to be so paranoid. Indeed the most severe criticism he actually received in the Commons was from Wakley who thought the Bill crude and carelessly drawn. It was his opinion, he said with his usual irony, that it must have been drawn by "some legal gentleman who was practising as an amateur."

To Lord Denman, on the Lords' third reading, deodands were a remnant of a barbarous and absurd law, but as they were the only security against death caused by reckless conduct their abolition was a strong argument in favour of the other Bill. When enacted, however, the Fatal Accidents Act provided quite inadequate compensation in most cases and meant that, after the abolition of deodands, the relatives of victims of railway accidents were left with few rights against the railway companies who could often rely on the defences of common employment and contributory negligence which had been no answer to deodands. It seems strange that Campbell thought the companies were hostile to Bills which were so advantageous to them.

Sir John Campbell was in fact another interesting character. He had gone to St. Andrew's University when only 11 years old and was called to the English Bar on November 15, 1806. He took silk in 1827, the year he was elected to the House of Commons for Stafford. The first Reform Bill of 1831 at first appeared to him to be too revolutionary, but he came to regard it as a prudent reform and voted for the second reading when it was carried by a majority of one. He became Attorney-General in 1834 and introduced a great deal of legislation. Later he wrote the *Lives of the Lord Chancellors* and *Lives of the Chief Justices* which, although eminently readable, are far from reliable. He was always an active law reformer, as statutes bearing his name testify, and in 1859 he was appointed Lord Chancellor at the age of 79.

Despite weaknesses in the deodand system its good features might well have been incorporated in Lord Campbell's Act. Indeed this seems to have been the view of J.A. Stuart-Wortley, a Tory backbencher in the Commons, who thought they exhibited advantages of being inexpensive, speedy and of universal application. But the intention was to destroy deodands, not improve them. On this occasion the powerful railway interests were to defeat Wakley although his concept of compensation was to succeed in the end. Curiously Wakley finally voted to end deodands (the voting was 51-6) probably because they were an arbitrary medieval survival and believing, with many others, that the Fatal Accidents Act would be an improvement. Indeed, he made it clear that he considered deodands to be in an unsatisfactory state where there could be liability without negligence. And he asked the government for an assurance that if the Act did not work well they would bring in another. Needless to say, no such assurance was given.

It might be asked if the Act really was an improvement upon the system it replaced. At the time undoubtedly it was not. However, it was itself capable of improvement whereas deodands were an insufficient measure of compensation being based solely upon the nature of the offending article and the quite arbitrary value placed upon it by a jury. It could not properly be related to the victim's injuries although juries sometimes managed to do something in this direction.

Deodands also had a curious parallel with the so-called penal compensation which, under the early Factories and Mines Act, magistrates could award to the victims of industrial accidents or their families. Following Bentham's concept of criminal compensation, these early statutes enabled the whole, or part, of a fine inflicted for breaches of their provisions to be applied as civil compensation in criminal proceedings. Local benches of magistrates frequently proved hostile to the scheme, but the concept was not abandoned until the Factories Act 1959. Since then, of course, magistrates and Judges have been given power to order a person convicted of an offence to pay compensation for any personal injury, loss or damage arising from his offence.

Leaving the House of Commons

On June 25, 1846 the third reading of Peel's Bill for repeal of the

Corn Laws was carried. During the same evening he was defeated by the "Combination" as it was called, led by Disraeli and Lord George Bentinck, by 73 votes on a Coercion Bill for Ireland. Daniel O'Connell and his friends, including Wakley, supported the one but, naturally, not the other. Indeed, Wakley had always opposed the rule of Ireland from Westminster. For them, repeal and free trade were an essential part of the struggle of the middle class to seize power from the aristocracy as Cobden and Bright never ceased to inform the large crowds at their great Anti-Corn Law rallies. The failure of the potato crop in Ireland with its disastrous famine had forced Peel's hand. But Catholic emancipation had already seriously weakened Peel and the Tories in 1829 and Peel's subsequent measures to assist the Irish short of the repeal of the Act of Union antagonized many of his supporters without winning friends among either the Radical or the Irish MPs.

Peel fell in consequence and a General Election was called for July. Samuel Warren, a lawyer and author, announced he would stand for Finsbury. This must have been seen as a serious threat since Wakley and Duncombe campaigned as never before. In the event Warren suddenly withdrew stating that most of his very influential supporters would be out of town or abroad. Wakley, still possessed of a biting tongue, retorted that if Warren had any influential friends abroad they were probably at Botany Bay. Wakley and Duncombe, standing on Chartist principles, went on to be once more returned unopposed.

Later in the year Wakley introduced a Bill for the registration of qualified medical practitioners and for amending the law relating to the practice of medicine. Although it was not enacted, since it contained penal clauses against quacks who still benefited from Whig approval of laissez-faire in medicine, this Bill was of enormous significance. It led to the appointment of a strong Select Committee which included Macaulay, who had written the Indian Penal Code singlehandedly, Sir James Graham and Wakley. Their labours were ultimately to result 12 years later in the important Medical Act of 1858. The fact that it was the seventeenth Bill dealing with the topic to have been presented to Parliament since 1840 - all previously unsuccessful - is a measure of Wakley's success. In fact, Wakley's exposures in the first 10 years of *The Lancet* had resulted in the first Select Committee on Medical Education and Practice in 1834. The vast amount of evidence given to the Committee had confirmed Wakley's indictment of the profession but much of it was lost when the House of Commons was destroyed by fire in October 1834. Bundles of manuscripts loosely tied up in window curtains were thrown out of windows to avoid the conflagration while, according to legend, Fellows of the Royal Colleges of Surgeons and Physicians desperately threw them back inside! In fact, Wakley believed the Royal Colleges had started the fire and that he was once again the victim of incendiarism.

Under Wakley's Bill no one would have been allowed to practice medicine unless properly qualified and registered. Otherwise they faced prosecution as would registered men who brought the profession into disrepute. His Bill also provided for uniformity of education and qualification. Naturally Wakley put up a strong fight for these reforms in the Select Committee whose deliberations were constantly delayed by the great medical corporations. In the end, however, the Act adopted many of Wakley's recommendations although it merely restricted quacks rather than outlawing them. And to accommodate the medical bodies it set up a General Council of Medical Education and Registration on which they were heavily represented. Nevertheless it was a landmark in medical thinking and practice whose beneficial effects are still with us today.

Wakley also spoke in favour of the Coroners Bill of 1851 which provided for coroners to be paid fixed salaries instead of fees based on the number of inquests held. When Lord Robert Grosvenor, as president of the English Homeopathic Association, alleged in the House that Wakley's son, Henry Membury Wakley, was an incompetent deputy coroner Wakley promptly denounced the Association as an "audacious set of quacks" who wanted to advertise themselves. For good measure he went on to call them "noodles and knaves, the noodles forming the majority and the knaves using them as tools". He then produced confirmation from the jury that on the only occasion complained of the deputy coroner had performed his duty in an able and impartial manner.

He also, in the same year, commenced to analyse a wide range of basic foods together with London water, tobacco and opium and publish the results in *The Lancet.* To further the work he set up the Lancet Analytical Sanitary Commission. Considerable publicity followed and within a few years Wakley achieved the astonishing result that adulteration of food was reduced by nine-tenths. He would not stop there, however, and before too long secured the appointment of a Select Committee which was followed in 1860 by a food adulteration statute. To this we owe the appointment of Public Analysts today. As usual his voice was effective in the best interests of the people.

Finally, in 1852, when Lord John Russell resigned and the Queen sent for Lord Derby to form a government, Wakley reluctantly decided to retire from the House of Commons following a serious collapse. He was an indefatigable worker. Long hours as editor of *The Lancet,* continual speaking and writing, and the arduous nature of his duties as coroner with frequent inquests over a large area as well as his duties in the House had taken their toll. His retirement was greeted with loud expressions of regret. His work in Parliament was widely known and was considered to have been a great success. In a lengthy estimate of Wakley, well worth quoting, G.H. Francis in his

Orators of the Age had written (1847):

> He has been a shrewd and constant observer of human
> nature in all grades and is not burdened with an
> overpowering sense of immaculate purity of public men. Still,
> you never hear from him those coarse charges of personal
> corruption against individuals which will often fall from Mr.
> Duncombe, notwithstanding his gentlemanly manners and
> superficial refinement ... and though he often indulges in
> sarcastic humour it seldom or never carries a venomous
> sting ... If he has not quite conquered the prejudices
> entertained towards Ultra-Radical intruders by men of birth
> and station he has at least made them feel his intellectual
> power and acknowledge his moral equality. In this respect he
> has done more to advance the interests of the millions by
> making their advocacy respectable than have many more
> flashy and showy popular leaders.
>
> Mr. Wakley has extraordinary energy both physical and
> mental. To see him bringing up his portly, bulky frame along
> the floor of the House of Commons, with swinging arms, and
> rolling, almost rollicking gait - his broad fair face inspired with
> good humour, and his massive forehead set off by light,
> almost flaxen hair, flowing in wavy freedom backwards
> around his head, and the careless ease of his manly yet half-
> boyish air, as though he had no thought or care beyond the
> impression or impulse of the moment; to watch the frank,
> hearty goodwill with which he greets his personal friends as
> he throws himself heedlessly into his seat, and interchanges
> a joke or an anecdote, or perhaps some stern remark on the
> passing scene, with those around, then, in a few minutes
> afterwards, rising to make, perhaps, some important motion,
> laying bare some gross case of pauper oppression, or taking
> up the cause of the medical practitioners with all the zeal of
> one still of the craft; to witness the freshness and vigour with

which he throws himself into the business before him, you would little guess the amount of wearying labour and excitement he had already gone through during the day; yet he has perhaps been afoot from the earliest hour, has perchance presided at more than one inquest during the morning, listening with a conscientious patience to the evidence, or taking part with an earnest partisanship in the case; then off as fast as horses could carry him down to the committee-rooms of the House of Commons, there to exhibit the same restless activity of mind, the same persevering acuteness, the same zeal and energy; and after hours, perhaps spent in his laborious duty, rendered still more irksome by a heated atmosphere and the intrigues of baffling opponents, returning home to accumulate the facts necessary for the exposure of some glaring abuse in the Post-office or the Poor Law Commission, or to manage the multifarious correspondence which his manifold public duties compel him to embark in. Yet such is often the daily life of this hard-working man: he is absolutely indefatigable; nothing daunts him, nothing seems to tire him.

J.F.Clarke, who knew Wakley well, also spoke of his voice of "considerable power and sweetness" in public speaking, and of his "genial good nature and wonderful animal spirits."

Despite his radicalism Wakley's "portly frame" was always well dressed in the manner of a gentleman of the times. His eyes were grey with a peculiarly penetrating and sagacious expression. He had a high forehead and a firm mouth and chin around which, in his older years, drooped a bushy white moustache. Although he allowed his hair to flow instead of wearing it in the fashionable short bob, he conformed to fashion in wearing a frock coat above tight trousers and short ankle boots. Under the coat he would often wear a brightly coloured waistcoat with velvet lapels and a high collar under a loosely knotted cravat. To *Punch* he was always something of a dandy, even a Tory, and an unlikely Radical. But, however improbable, the verdict on his radicalism is crystal clear.

Conclusion

It has to be said that Wakley's family life left something to be desired. Because he was so busy in public life he always found in his home a quiet haven of rest. This also suited his wife who was a shy, retiring woman but understandably she wished his absences had been less frequent. For her he was too restless and the champion of too many causes. Moreover, she was out of sympathy with the stand he took on many issues and his entry into Parliament caused her much grief. To some extent this was the consequence of financial worries. She plainly thought the heavy expense of publishing *The Lancet* quite enough for one man and the disputes in which he engaged in its columns sufficient too. Yet they managed to live happily and in some splendour in their two homes at Bedford Row and Harefield Park, although it remains true that at most times Wakley's expenditure exceeded his income. Yet, as befits a doctor, he did not smoke and drank very little, although the dangers of such indulgences were, of course, not known at the time even to doctors. In any event, whatever the underlying reason, Wakley's wife did not share her husband's enthusiasms, distrusted public life and blamed it for separating them. At length, she died at Brighton in 1857 after a long illness.

The couple had one daughter, who died when a child, and three sons, Thomas Henry, Henry Membury and James Goodchild. To them Wakley was an indulgent father although, again, he spent too little time with them. Nonetheless, they were all successful when they grew up. The eldest, as the son of a well-known Radical, found life at Oxford uncongenial and was withdrawn from Wadham College and placed at the less restrictive University of London. He later became senior proprietor of *The Lancet* whilst the youngest, Dr. James Goodchild Wakley, was to succeed his father as editor. Henry Membury had become deputy-coroner under his father but was more concerned to practise as a barrister, on which no known view of his father is recorded.

Home life for the family was undoubtedly sociable. Wakley was a popular host at Bedford Square and Harefield Park and he often spent time at the latter shooting with his sons to their great delight. His guests came from many walks of life and political positions. His many friends included Count D'Orsay, Charles Dickens, Tom Duncombe, Thomas Attwood, Feargus O'Connor, Lord Brougham and Daniel O'Connell. He was a man who drove himself with tremendous energy. He worked 15 or 16 hours a day which often included travelling by horse or coach 60 or more miles, holding inquests into numerous tragedies, sitting on parliamentary committees, attending debates into the early hours, as well as editing *The Lancet.* In 1851 the consequences reared their head. He started the day at Harefield at sunrise, held seven inquests at different venues and attended the House of Commons until after midnight when he left to go to work on *The Lancet.* Outside the door of his office he collapsed and was found lying unconscious by a policeman. His consequent resolve to relax more led, as we have seen, to his retirement from Parliament, although he continued as coroner.

The decision to retire was undoubtedly beneficial since it was not until nine years later, in the winter of 1860, that he began to spit blood and weaken more seriously. In the following winter he went to stay in Brighton under the care of the same physician who had treated his wife. He enjoyed the Brighton air and responded to treatment sufficiently to be able to return to London in the spring. Here he resumed his duties as coroner but he was soon ill again with pulmonary tuberculosis, and on medical advice travelled to Madeira in October. There he lived in a small house in a climate he found congenial. His active mind was unabated and he quickly interested himself in the island. He made plans to import various English fruit trees, the grafts of which were sent to him, and typically he was soon promising to expose the fraudulent Madeira wine trade immediately on his return to England. In fact, he made arrangements to return on May 24, 1862 but on May 11, having returned from a sailing trip, he slipped on the beach. This trifling accident brought on a severe haemorrhage of the lungs from which he died peacefully five days later. So ended a tempestuous life.

Wakley's body was returned to England, in the packet boat "Comet", and he was buried on June 14 alongside his wife and daughter in the catacombs of Kensal Green Cemetery where his name may still be found. Nearby is a flamboyant temple in which the remains of John St. John Long, his enemy of earlier times, lie buried. The style of the cemetery reveals the influence of that great architect John Nash which may account for its popularity at one time with relatives of the well-known. At all events, among many others, Wakley's neighbours in death include Joseph Hume, Feargus O'Connor, Sydney Smith, Thackeray, Trollope, Thomas Hood, James Leigh Hunt, Wilkie Collins, Thomas Barnes, Emile Blondin, Isambard Brunel and George Cruikshank. If only their shades could enjoy each other's company!

SELECTED BIBLIOGRAPHY

The use of numerous notes has been avoided, but all quotations and matters of research have their source in the material set out in the Bibliography.

A. Manuscript Sources

(1) *British Museum Additional Mss.*
Place Papers: 27,790, 27,791, 27,796, 27,828, 35,149.
Peel Papers: 40,530, 40,549.

(2) *Public Record Office*
H.O.40/29, 44/6, 44/24, 44/25.
Wellington Despatches, 2nd ser. (1878).

B. Reports and Collections

Hansard (1834-58).
The Newgate Calendar (1820-24).

C. Contemporary Books, Newspapers, Journals and Pamphlets

The Annual Register (1836).
Clarke, J.F., *Autobiographical Recollections of the Medical Profession* (1874).
Cobbett, Wm., *Weekly Political Register* (1820).
Dickens, Charles, "Some Recollections of Immutability," *Reprinted Pieces* (1906).
Eliot, George, *Middlemarch* (1871).
The Examiner, (1846).

Francis, G.H., *Orators of the Age* (1847).

Gammage, R.C. *History of the Charist Movement, 1837-1854* (1854).

Gardiner, W., *Facts Relative to the Late Fire and Attempt to Murder Mr. Wakley* (1820).

The *Gentleman's Magazine* (1862).

The *Lancet* (1823-65).

The *Law Magazine* (1867).

The *Law Review* (1845-6).

Lovett, Wm., *The Life and Struggles of William Lovett* (1876).

Lovelace, George. *The Victims of Whiggery.* (1837)

The *Poor Man's Guardian* (1831-32).

Punch (1841-42).

A Report on the Trial, Cooper v. Wakley etc. (1829).

A Report of the Trial, etc. (1829).

Rogers, George, "Letter to Thomas Wakley Esq. M.P.", November 1837.

The *Sunday Times* (1830).

The *Times* 1820, 1831-32, 1846.

Wakley, Thomas, "A Letter to the People of England on the New Project for Gagging the Press", April 1836.

The *Westminster Review* (1824).

D. Modern Books, Journals and Articles

Bostetter, Mary, "The Journalism of Thomas Wakley", *The Study of Mass Media and Communications,* No. 5.

Brook, C., *Battling Surgeon* (1945).

Thomas Wakley, (1962).

Butler, J.R.M., *The Passing of the Great Reform Bill* (1914).

Cawthorn, Elisabeth, "Thomas Wakley and the Medical Coronership - Occupational Death and the Judicial Process", 30 *Medical History* (1986).

Dean, Phyllis, *The First Industrial Revolution* (1965).

Dickson, R., "The Tolpuddle Martyrs. Guilty or Not Guilty?" 7 *Journal of Legal History* (1986).

Dictionary of National Biography.

Froggatt, Sir Peter, "Thomas Wakley, The Lancet and the Surgeons", 7 *Journal of the Irish College of Physicians and Surgeons* (1977).

"The Lancet: Wakley's Instrument for Medical Education Reform", 29 *Journal of the Society of Occupational Medicine* (1979).

Hostettler, John, "The Movement for Reform of the Criminal Law in England in the 19th Century", *University of London Ph.D. Thesis* (1982).

"Thomas Wakley - An Enemy of Injustice", 5 *Journal of Legal History* (1984).

The Politics of Criminal Law - Reform in the Nineteenth Century (1992).

Linebaugh, Peter, "The Tyburn Riot Against the Surgeons", in *Albion's Fatal Tree* (1975).

Marlow, Joyce, *The Tolpuddle Martyrs* (1971).

McMenemy, W.H., 1 *Lancet* (1962).

Newman, Charles, *The Evolution of Medical Education in the Nineteenth Century* (1957).

Pollock and Maitland, *The History of English Law,* ii (1895).

Reader, W.J., *Professional Men. The Rise of the Professional Classes in 19th Century England* (1966).

Richardson, Ruth, *Death, Dissection and the Destitute* (1987).

Roberts, David, "How Cruel was the Victorian Poor Law?" 6 *Historical Journal* (1963).

Smith, Harry, "From Deodand to Dependency", 11 *American Journal of Legal History* (1967).

Sprigge, Sir S. Squire, *The Life and Times of Thomas Wakley* (1897).

Stanhope, John, *The Cato Street Conspiracy* (1962).

Thurston, Gavin, "A Queer Sort of Thing", 37 *Medico-Legal Journal* (1969).
Wallas, Graham, *The Life of Francis Place* (1918).

INDEX